SOLE TO SOUL

HOW TO LOVE AND HEAL

BY

ARIEL A. TALMOR

i

Sole to Soul: How to Love and Heal
Copyright © by Ariel A. Talmor

For information:
Ariel A. Talmor, 3245 University Avenue Suite #1315,
San Diego, CA 92104

PRINTED IN THE UNITED STATES OF AMERICA

Visit our website at www.soletosoulhowtoloveandheal.com

Book cover design by SMAK

Disclaimer: All material is the opinion of the author. There is no attempt to provide medical or psychological advice. The author cannot assume responsibility for any personal interpretation of the contents. If in doubt, seek professional advice. All names used herein are fictitious; any resemblance to real people is random.

First Edition 2012

ISBN: 9780615616797

This book is dedicated to
all my clients and students,
who opened their hearts
and minds to me and helped me
on my own spiritual path.

It is thanks to you
that this book was made possible.

Thank you!

With love,

– Ariel A. Talmor

CONTENTS

~Preface~

~Part I: SOLE: Footsteps along the Universal Path~

~Part II: SOUL:
Our Density & Our Destiny~

~Part III: INTEGRATION: All One & All Right~

~Part IV: APPENDICES~

~Part IV: APPENDICES – Continued~

~Part IV: Glossary and Index~

~Preface~

Important Notes from the Author

Having observed many patients and given numerous lectures, I often asked myself "What are the principles in mind-body medicine that guide self discovery and healing as pertaining to my Sole to Soul point of view?" I compiled many pages of material, diagrams and comparisons that assisted me in passing the knowledge to my college students and clients. As my classes evolved with time, the body of material grew gradually reaching a point where my students asked often to put it all into a book. They typically commented that in my reflexology classes they learned about themselves and felt it was a highly spiritualized class that allowed them to take a deep look at their lives and the way they acted, thought and felt.

I realized that I want to reach more people. I sat down to compile this body of work.

Over the course of writing this book I met many wonderful people. I would like to thank Michael Martin for his inspiration, Alex Phillips, Evelyn Mendoza, Rich Guy Miller the Coffee Man, Eddie Kaddi, the gifted graphic designer, Mark Holguin for his support and Christy Johnson, my editor whose input was very instrumental.

Suggestions to My Readers

This is not a typical "how to" manual, rather it is a flowing text, with much information, which explores various aspects of the human experience in connection with the physical reality and the Universe. The reader will learn valuable principles for better living, from various angles, that address universal life lessons. This book is rich with analogies, stories and information. At times, new words that I have come up with are used to convey new thought patterns, e.g. "is-ness" – the way thing just are. It is about the journey that follows the road to soul-based and self realized living. In Shirley MacLaine's book *The Camino,* she encounters along her pilgrimage to Spain a reflexologist who relates to the sole-soul connection. He explains to her about "The healing of reflexology, which uses pressure upon the meridian points of the feet to release blocked energy and blocked memories. When the energy is released, health resulted." He adds that "Health is also knowing your memories."

I have composed this book to take you through a similar experience of having a series of healing sessions with me. In these sessions, there is ample interaction both verbal and physical. The text pertains to many aspects of health on all levels. Keep yourself in mind as you read through the stories, anecdotes and thoughts I've compiled throughout the years. Allow what you have read to assist you on your path to self discovery.

How to Use This Book

My goal is to help you rediscover what matters to you and how to attain it. It is also my intention to inspire you to connect your conscious living with your subconscious living so that you can live a more integrated and fuller life. Read the book through once, absorbing what you can. Start a journal and write down any responses or questions you have to the text, noting the page number and date with each entry. Then go back to the parts that you would like to explore. Choose one idea at a time and reflect on it for a while. Then move on to the next idea. Each small step matters and each connection you make toward understanding is a success.

You will find each of the Charts, Exercises and Lists in the Appendix Section. They are there so that you can easily refer to them at any time. Also, I have included a very extensive Glossary of Terms and Index of Words to help you quickly find what is important to you. My hope is that you will use this book as a reference book for living a more positive life. Perhaps after reading it through—you will every once in a while think about it or see it on your bookshelf, pick it up, open it to a "random" page, read a passage and apply it to your current situation. "Random" reading can be very powerful. This is how you heal along your spiritual path.

Who Can Heal Along Their Spiritual Path?

Walking is a physical act of alignment and direction. Metaphysically speaking, the path we walk on, which is our life direction, is the result of our beliefs and thoughts. To improve the choice of path, we must bring more energetic flow to it. When we are healed we walk in perfect alignment with energy and matter.

Everything seems to happen at the right place and the right time. When we are healed we walk humbly in synchronicity with nature. Along our path we visit many "stations" that teach us the exact lessons needed for growth. When we are healing we live in the present and move forward with ease. People, places and circumstances – all seem to be there for the right reasons. When we are aware of the flow in our life and accordingly the wonder that accompanies it then we are more aware of the healing that occurs along the way.

Introduction

Recall the most pleasant walk you've ever taken. Imagine the birds singing, the fresh air cooling you on a beautiful day and the joy and comfort you experience in living and walking for that exact moment. Visualize the path you are walking as your entire life. Understand that every moment of your life can be as calming and enjoyable as what you feel on this walk.

There is a prominent metaphysical statement that says "As above – so below." This quote appears on the Tabula Smaragdina or the Emerald Tablet which is a philosophical text related to Alexander the Great. This tablet is one of the earliest works of alchemy in the world, aiming to explain the secret of the primordial substance. It has been examined and theorized upon throughout history by brilliant minds such as Isaac Newton, Paracelsus, Roger Bacon and others.

One of the lines of the Tabula Smaragdina clearly states "That which is Below corresponds to that which is Above and that which is Above, corresponds to that which is Below", oftentimes summarized as simply: "As above, so below." This principle also appears in Kabbalistic texts. I have reflected on this concept for a long time. The human body is the microcosm: it is a reflection of the entire Universe. This connection is a key to understanding our life. This book draws on universal truths, but it caters to all, including those with a religious perspective, or who have a perception of "god" on some level. It's important to note that since man is created "in the image of god," this image is a mirror of the energies that exist throughout the human body and the Universe: As above, so below.

In the human body, the head represents the higher self, the infinite. The feet are at the other end of the body and therefore represent the 'opposite' of the infinite, the here and now or the Earth. We can also say that while the head represents everything that is out of sight, or the symbolic endless dimension of existence, the feet correspond to the apparent and planet Earth. Hence, just like the head represents the unknown, out of reach aspect of our being (symbolically speaking), so do the feet ground and anchor us to the here and now.

Throughout the book there are certain terms that are mentioned frequently. The *Ego* is referred to as a part of us that is limited and fear-based. It inflicts suffering due to its contractive nature. It is similar to the *Pain body*, which is the memory we carry from perceived unresolved conflicts. The *Higher self* is our true self, our love-based part that seeks expansion through unity and growth. These terms and others are presented from various angles so that you, the reader, can use them as working tools on your journey.

Sole to Soul is a journey outlining the connection between us and the Universe. It is a glimpse upon the path you are walking in this life and will assist you in taking the scenic route on your way to self-realization thus aiding in the healing along your spiritual path.

~Part I: SOLE:
Footsteps on the Universal Path~

Chapter One:
Universal Oneness

Rediscovering the Soul through the Sole

At times, in the midst of our daily routines, it may be difficult to remember the spiritual connection inherent in our lives. Keeping simple principles in mind will enable us to stay tuned into the Universe and keep our focus. The infinite versus the here and now can be seen as "Heaven vs. Earth." When we say "Earth" we also refer to everything that takes place in the material world: It may be people, plants, furniture or water – to name some. This can be simply stated as "the world of forms." This is the world in which we usually live – 99% of what we see around us.

The world of forms is when we see an object and we do not see the energy and context that connects to it – nor feel or know it. It is a state of perceived separation, despite the fact that all matter is tied to energy. It can be said that the world of forms, or matter, corresponds to the ego aspect of the self while the energy world corresponds to the higher self. This is a linear dimension where objects, living creatures or events "exist" with little or no connection to energy source. In reality, this dimension does not exist. It does exist however in our perception therefore it exists within our limited ego-identification with reality. Ego always implies a state of separation while the higher self is the gateway to a state of unification.

In other words, all it takes is to accept the hidden dimension, at least as a possibility. This hidden dimension is the 1 percent of what we see which is actually 99 percent of reality. What we don't normally see is the majority of existence. The naked eye sees a very limited part of what is truly going on around us. In some dogmas one is rarely encouraged to explore and / or ask many questions beyond the world around them. For example in Judeo-Christianity and other cultures there exists the story of "The Garden of Eden." Eden is a metaphor for the general human condition and its need to reverse the physical world back into metaphysical awareness. It is a story of choosing matter over energy and their balance thereof. The story of the "Garden of Eden" is about the fall from one dimension to another, from energy into matter. Having had this "fall" take place we are now in a position where we can engage in a process of reversal where we reconcile the world of matter with that of energy. This is the fall from infinity to linearity. It is a collective event that we all share, the primordial "sin." At the same time, we all have the tools to correct this fall by connecting with our higher selves.

It is not an accident that the Old Testament begins with the story of creation and shortly after describes the fall from Eden – the setting in which we have lived ever since. It's difficult to overlook the symbolic role ego played in the fall from Eden.

Our goal is to embrace energy, while monitoring the ego.

This action of falling symbolizes the gravity forces that go hand in hand with our perceptions of time and space. Eden can be seen as a symbolic multi-dimensional reality where one loses the connection with the Source by becoming linear, oblivious to the oneness that is the only true reality. One of the main focuses of any faith is regaining something that is lost; namely rekindling the connection to the Divine and, some say, to re-enter the kingdom of heaven, to repent a sin. This aspiration of re-gaining can be equated with the need to re-connect with lost energy, to regain the missing gateway to a reality beyond the mundane. Life is incomplete unless we cease to perceive reality as a linear plateau where time and space reign. Falling from Eden is merely a symbolic description of allowing gravity (ego) to take over; it is a choice to identify with the ego and thus look away from the higher self, our connection to the Source.

The Source can be given many names such as god, nature or the Universe, but the thread that unifies us with the Source is the fact that the Source is interconnectedness itself. This is the reason why we call our Universe by that name. The hint is right there – there is "one version" or "one frequency" for it all – UNI VERSE. Energy marries matter! This is what we call interconnectedness: everything resonates with everything, as if everything came from the same oneness. Because everything connects to everything, if we elect to see a form independent of its energy counterpart, we create a separation of energy from matter. This separation is artificial and only exists as much as we allow it to. That's right – if we chose to intend to see the interconnectedness we will gradually notice it and eventually live it. We will feel it.

Another way to look at this separation is to observe the gap that exists between our body and soul. In each and every one of us, gravity took its toll. The more gravity present in our life, the less connected we are. A great illustration for gravity is our own feet. The feet are a part of the body that is very dense due to its location in the body and its symbolic direct contact with Earth. On the other side of the body lies the head. The head has a symbolic lightness to it as it connects to the Universe. To live a full life, we need not only to reconcile energy and matter, but also to reconcile the head and the feet, so that universal energies can flow through us as if we are clear conduits.

Conducting Energy

Practically speaking, we are all conduits of energy. Energy enters the body though the feet, as well as through the head. The head is in touch with the higher frequency levels that are abundant in the Universe. It serves like an aerial, an antenna. In order to be in perfect shape this energy has to go through our bodies and ground itself to Earth through the feet. We want to be least resistant to energy flow by aspiring to have our energy centers, or Chakras, open. Our energetic flow lays in the way we reconcile polarities. Our ability to flow depends on how we deal with conflicts. If we resist dealing with conflicts they will tend to manifest in our bodies as disease.

**Every irritation we manifest
is an inside process that
could not express itself otherwise.**

The more aware we become of our inner desires, aspirations, attachments and fears, the more we can reconcile and relate to our inner self, so as not to need to manifest conflict in our body. This is the perfect flow that connects "above" (higher self) and "below" (physical body). Yet, if the "below" becomes too dense, the energy cannot flow through the body and the feet and an imbalance is formed. Energy from the Universe is hindered on its way through the body and the more density it meets the more hindrance there is.

Almost every organ has some correspondence to our consciousness. For example, the eyes represent our ability to truly see, beyond that which is in front of us. The correspondence of each of our organs is projected onto the feet through the force of gravity. The energy in the Universe flows vertically. The feet are the last point in the body that energy goes through. When energy is blocked from flowing through us, our feet become the densest part of the body. An energy blockage in the feet can manifest as either "crystals" (a combination of various waste materials), physical deformities or many other change in the feet. Any change in the feet could show us that we aren't allowing universal energy to flow freely through us. Not all changes are bad, but here we refer to deviations from the "perfect feet."

As we attempt to unblock or correct these deviations we allow flow of energy and, consequently, rectifications of those "misunderstandings." For example, when a person has many crystals over the pancreas reflex it could denote some frustration that prevents a person from self-realization and self love. There is a striking similarity in the Hebrew language between the word for pancreas and the word for heart. They both have exactly the same consonants: LV is for heart, LVLV is for pancreas. The pancreas represents the ultimate "marriage" between the spiritual and the physical worlds. It is because it regulates sugar which by itself is an equivalent to love. Love is the ultimate "glue" that affects all our realities – the physical and the non-physical.

Another interesting observation of the energy / matter conflict is the connection between energy and our higher self, as well as the connection between matter and our ego self. The more we identify with our egos, the more density will be present in our body. Our body is dense to begin with, being made of flesh and bones. Add to it ego resistance and we get a "real" density (it is only as real as our perception allows it to be). As the feet are the densest points in the human body, this is where our ego resistance will manifest the most. As the mechanism of more ego identification--that leads to more body density--occurs, more and more density accumulates in our feet. We become more and more dominated by this gravity. We also become more and more identified with the matter aspect of life. In this state, it is hard to feel enlightenment and live an integrated life. Consequently, on the body level, our feet start to show signs of fatigue and it becomes harder to "walk here." Remember that our feet reflect the four elements of the universe (Air, Fire, Water and Earth) and how well we flow with these elements.

Chapter Two:
The Elements

The Four Elements, The Five Elements

In traditional Astrology we use The Four Elements of Air, Fire, Water and Earth. In traditional Chinese medicine we use The Five Elements of Metal, Fire, Water, Earth and Wood. All these elements are present in the human body and the feet. The Four Elements represent universal energies whereas The Five Elements connect more to the human experience. I often wondered which set of elements is more important to work with: the Four or the Five. I realized that, when used together, their power is multiplied to be greater than one or the other alone.

While The Four Elements pertain to the universe and our connection to it, The Five Elements represent the human existence.

Both sets of elements represent different aspects of our existence. In other words, each of The Four Elements is found in the universe and is also present in our personalities and daily experiences. The Five Elements do not necessarily relate to the connection of the universe as much as to the processes within our bodies and in relation to our thoughts and feelings.

It is by combining the Four and Five Element Systems we will have a broader view of the human experience. Literally, if we add 4 and 5 together we get 9 and in Numerology 9 represents completion. In combining these two sets of elements—the 4 elements and the 5 elements—we can better understand the human experience in a more complete universal context.

The Four Elements

The Four Elements are entryways or gates to a dimension of universal truth, the oneness. See Appendix I for The Four Elements Chart of the Feet.

The Air Element – Senses and Sensibility

The Air element is the lightest of all elements. It is our connection with all that is above hence its vulnerability is the highest. It is most vulnerable to density – the more density we have the less the Air can manifest in us. It is infinite.

**Air is the most important element
because we need and use it the most.**

In the feet, the Air element is in our toes. If Air is unable to flow into the "energetically jammed" body, it starts to create toe deformities. Almost any deformity in the toes is correctable through repetitive manipulation. We want to allow the toes to be better receivers of energy by opening them up. Any change in the toes may denote a basic change in the flow and receptivity for the entire body. For instance, if there is too much dry skin on the toes it could be that the Earth element took over the Air. This often happens when we live with many "shoulds" in our life. It's hard to be a free thinker when our Air is covered with Earth!

Observing peoples toes can teach us how well they live within their Air element. The Air is a masculine element that thrives on heat which comes from the Fire element based on the ball of the foot. The Air has to be light just like the Fire is hot, the Water is wet and the Earth is dense. Remember that the Air element is opposed to the Earth element, the "above and below" of it all. There is a natural tension between these poles which presents a need for balance.

Air is a positive element, light blue in color. It contains our many senses. Through this element we receive information that we arrange in our conceptual space. All communication passes through the Air element - intelligence, intuition, and intellect - all of these are among its attributes. Air conforms to and encompasses all the other elements, can sweep things in its wake, can confuse, distract or delude. It represents forgetfulness, flightiness, impatience and the need for change. This element is patterns, principles, mind, conscious theories, explanations, rhetoric, writing and dreaming.

Many of us have some blockage in the Air element because all the other elements pass through this one therefore potentially causing a bottleneck effect. Contained in the Air element are all the thought patterns and reflections we've had in our lives. We all tend to suffer from too much energy in the head and too little energy in the feet. This makes us ungrounded and caught up in compulsive repetitive thinking.

The Air element is also the link to our higher self. It means that we chose to act from a restrictive and linear point of reference, as opposed to a vast one. Some people feel they are just fine with what there is. They are content with things being as they are. They may also feel that there is a great sacrifice in allowing the higher self to intervene in their daily lives. This fear is understandable. At the same time, remember that fear is the ego's language. Through fear, the ego endorses our gravity and suffering. Many people are afraid to gradually shift their ego perception as they link it to their name, identity or possessions.

The idea is that one is to integrate, to allow in – to become fully who we are. This integration manifests itself in the body as toes that are straight forward, thus receptive, like antennas that are open to receive broadcasts from the universe.

The Fire Element – Passion in Action

The Fire element corresponds to the chest cavity and is located on the ball of the foot. It relates to the muscular system. In this region oxygen burns and enriches the body thus heating and providing energy. Fire is a masculine, positive, dynamic element. It seeks ways to expand and grow. It represents passion, ambition, courage and a lack of consideration. It is difficult and dominant. Fire is extroverted and reaches out. This element represents the ego and the internal power of the personality.

Fire seeks to expand its territory and influence. Fire is a consuming element that seeks to burn and dissolve what gets in its way. Fire is the ignition of the soul without which true love would not be possible. Just like within a motor's engine, Fire fuels the movement. Fire is quick decisions and swift actions. It is hope and optimism. It is the most giving of all elements. When we enter this gate we are able to love passionately and unconditionally. At the same time this gate leads us to the ultimate shrine of the ego and the "I." In the solar system the sun is Fire. If there was a single planet that we needed for survival it would be the sun, therefore there is a magical and mystical quality about Fire well embedded in our subconscious and psyche.

The Water Element – The Ocean of Emotions

The Water element invites us to delve into the emotional realm. It resides in the abdomen and the arch area of the foot. Water corresponds to our kidneys, blood and bladder. Water gives the reason for living in that feelings move us and allow us to go deep into our souls. Water forms solutions and dreams, intuition and gut feelings. Water is a feminine element mysterious and profound. With Water we absorb what others are feeling. There is an assertion that the intestines contain as many neurons as the brain. In this respect Water is our subconscious mind; the one that has the answers and primordial knowledge.

The Water element reflects our ongoing emotional state (as opposed to a momentary emotional state). The lower we descend on the arch area, the deeper the emotions become and the less accessible those emotions become. Since energy cannot just fade to nowhere, when we process emotions, we sometimes fail to fully do so. For example, under stress and fear we tend to 'shove' the emotions "under the carpet." Therefore, any emotion that is not processed will end up in our lower abdomen which is in the low Water element area. The "sunken" emotions can only go so far down in the abdomen, as the abdominal floor marks its namesake – a floor. Therefore, unprocessed emotions gradually accumulate on the floor. Having nowhere to go, they form a layer of density.

Often, the client may have unpleasant dreams following manipulation of this area of the foot. It's very important to clear this area so that the energy flows evenly in our bodies. Since this area is just above the Earth element area on the foot, it will push the person to feel trapped because it can't pass through the solidity of Earth.

The Earth Element – Grounded by Gravity

The Earth element is in the lowest part of the body and is the heaviest element. It corresponds to our pelvis and the heel of our foot. Earth is a stable, grounded element that draws on sensuality, permanence, sexuality, fertility and the survival instinct. It is dominated by gravity, money, possessions, greed - all correspond to this element.

Earth ties to the basic instincts of survival: food, sleep and sex.

The heel is the Earth element. Here, we want to see some coarseness (dry skin) as it means our Earth is grounded. Similarly, in severe health situations, such as cancer or chronic disease, we often observe a heel which is mushy and lacks in firmness.

In all, the feet will show the state of The Four Elements in our life. This means that each element will present its condition by itself and in relation to the other three elements. For example, if the Fire or Passion in Action area is puffy it could be "filled with air." You guessed right, too much thinking and too little action.

Each element on our feet connects with the same element in our life. This is because each part of the foot connects to the whole body which in turn connects with the entire Universe. Our goal is to flow in such a way that we allow all the elements to manifest harmoniously in our life. We want to be like a tree whose upper branches aspire to the infinite high above (AIR), yet its roots are deep in the ground (EARTH). Sustenance (WATER) is abundant and sun (FIRE) is present as life-giving energy.

The Five Elements

The Five Elements appear in similar forms in many Eastern cultures, and correspond to different types of energy in constant interaction that reflects our thinking, habits, instincts and emotions. The Five Elements are Metal, Fire, Water, Earth and Wood. While The Four Elements form horizontally on the feet, The Five Elements form vertically. Each line between the toes represents the border between the elements. The 5 elements also involve body systems, so they become more intricate in their dispersion. However, from the toe point of view, we can safely say that The Five Elements form clearly under each toe. See Appendix II for The Toe Reading Chart.

The Metal Element – It's All in Our Head?
   The Metal element connects to our thinking and perception.
The Fire Element – It's Practically a Habit
   The Fire element connects to our habits and practicality.
The Water Element – Instinctual Boundaries
   The Water element connects to our instincts and boundaries.
The Earth Element - Earthly Emotions
   The Earth element connects to our emotions.
The Wood Element – Cultivating Creativity
   The Wood element corresponds to our creativity and sexuality.

Identifying Your Elemental Imbalances

I've witnessed several patterns of elemental imbalances in my clinical experience. Ideally, all elements should be present in our lives and flowing harmoniously with one another. By improving elemental balance we improve synchronicity and vitality in our life.

You can discover a key ingredient in your mind-body health through the Elemental Imbalances Quiz. It was created to help you to discover where the imbalances lie within you. You will find these helpful tools in the Appendices:
Elemental Imbalances Quiz – Appendix III
Scoring & Analysis of the Quiz – Appendix IV
Elemental Balancing Exercises – Appendix V

Chapter Three:
Universal Wisdom

Dreams and Reflexology

Many people have excessive dreaming after their feet are treated in a reflexology session. This is part of the process of allowing the ego (feet / Earth) to give way to the higher self (head / Air). Removing density from the feet allows for higher frequency (less density) to flow in. As we remove density from our feet, energy can flow better to us. It is like a tune up or, even better, an alignment. Our higher selves have it all lined up for us. It is through density and resistance to change that we become "poorly incarnated."

Incarnation is a union of energy and matter.

One of the greatest mediums through which we can observe the changes we go through in foot work is the dreaming process.

15

Dreaming is such an important part of life that it shows up in religious prophecy, as in Joseph's dream interpretation about the seven year famine and Jacob's dream about the ladder to heaven. In our sleep, our ego moves aside and allows the higher self to come through ("ego" as in the context of the active mind). It is not that we have the ability to customize a dream necessarily, but we certainly get clues for our unfolding reality as we dream.

There are two fundamental questions in relation to dreaming that stem from two opposing presumptions as to the origin of dreams. The first being, "does the dream originate in the person himself?" and the other "is it a symbolic message from an external source?" The common denominator for the dream perception of Sigmund Freud, Carl Jung and others is that the essence of the dream is a reflection of the individual's subconscious mind. The differences in their approaches stem from the difference in the perception of the subconscious. Freud's innovation in dream perception is that a dream expresses forbidden and repressed desires of the individual, especially those pertaining to violence and sexuality. He theorized that dreams reflect these desires through sublime mechanisms of symbolism. Jung sees the dream as an expression for the collective unconscious and therefore there are also collective dreams common to all humanity from which we can learn about the pan-human archetypes. According to Jung those are the more meaningful dreams loaded with mythological motifs. From this standpoint the Jungian approach is closer to the perception of a dream as a conduit to external messages than the Freudian approach.

In traditional dream understanding, a person participates while asleep - in unification of actual reality and external symbolic reality. Some messages in our dreams reflect on the evolution of our life condition. Every one of our dreams could be seen as a message of premonitory value. Many of my clients have had symbolic dreams. Some contain numerical values (numbers 1, 3, 7 are very frequent), animals (serpents, spiders and fish, to name few popular ones) or objects (for example: house, car, piano). It is interesting to note that the house almost always represents the seat of our soul whereas the car represents our current life journey.

Very often dreaming means there is a healing process in action. Any powerful encounter can yield an onset of dreams with a great depth of meaning. Our objective is to connect with our dreams. Get a book about dreams and keep it near your bed. Keep your journal and pen or pencil nearby, and when you wake up, you can write an excerpt from what you remember. Write your dreams with dates and underline keywords. It is very uplifting to go through our daily awake-life and draw parallels with the symbolism from our nightly dream-life.

"Jay" is a fifty year old male, a very left brain person – analytical and pragmatic. A software engineer and a cyclist, Jay came to me with the intention to open up and integrate his life. We started with a weekly meeting. After about fifteen sessions Jay told me that he had an interesting dream. In the dream he was on a desert-like volcanic island. There were some palm trees there and a big imposing volcano in the background. Jay was surrounded by some unfamiliar friendly people.

There was a small bonfire in their midst. The backdrop of his dream is a great example of how The Four Elements play into our lives. In Jay's dream all The Four Elements were present. He recalled glancing at the blue sky or Air element, the bonfire was naturally the Fire element, the surrounding water is of course the Water element and the soil of the island is the Earth element. My suggestion to Jay was to look at these elements and how they reflect his life.

Dreaming of The Four Elements is a sign that Jay is processing and attaining some inner equilibrium. The island amidst the vast ocean is a symbol of how Jay is aware of his emotional world (Water). Yet he still stands on solid ground (Earth). Within the space of the island there is Fire - his passion, his "ignition" is still present. The dark blue sky (Air)--which is a projection of the ocean—his mental / intellectual world, is in harmony with his emotions (Water).

This dream is a reflection of some adjustment and moving into a newer state where Jay's subconscious is more awake. One can also say that Jay woke up to realize the vastness of his emotional scope - in his dream the ocean is open and defines the island's size. The ocean paints the sky blue, yet it allows for the presence of fire on the island - the water does not extinguish the fire.

In our life-long process of release, dreaming is very important. Dreaming reaches far into the energy realm in an attempt to reconcile the worlds and allow more balance. To induce better recollection and connection to dreams, rubbing your feet can be very beneficial as it grounds you and opens soul portals at the same time – sole to soul. Therefore, every time you feel confused, listless or just ungrounded, rub your feet (or have someone else do it for you). It will surely induce more clarity and subconscious activity, even if you still can't remember your actual dreams.

A simple foot rub does wonders to our clarity of mind.

The scientific and artistic natures of our life connect to the left and right hemispheres of our brain. The left hemisphere is "science" and the right hemisphere is "art." It is similar to Yin (feminine/art/non-linear) and Yang (masculine/science/linear): The separation of Yin and Yang still implies that it is only through the unified dance of Yin and Yang that true oneness exists. This distinction between polarities is only for learning purposes. True existence doesn't imply that we should work from the left side of the brain now and the right side later. It implies being both at once.

Remember the polarity connection between the feet and the head. When we rub our feet we are not merely performing a foot rub we are actually reaching the other polarity, the head. Each pole feeds the other side and when we attain circulation in our feet we

18

affect the hemispheric balance for clearer thinking. One of the most common traits of all my clients after a session is that--beyond the relaxation and general feelings of well being--they reported a sense of clarity as if the chatter in their head subsided. They once again could see themselves as a part of the Universe in absolute clarity.

Clarity is essential for understanding and is essential to removing stumbling blocks that stand in the way to self knowledge. It is like removing beliefs and perceptions that block the knowledge of who we truly are. In healing, we often draw on the body's ability to heal. We are not reinventing the wheel; we are just spinning it, getting it going. Ideally, we do not need any intervention, but sometimes because of stress we slow down and we do need an external intervention to spin our wheel. In other words, to remind us of whom we are and that we are fully alive now.

Know Your Zodiac Sign, Know Your Stress Area

Stress is a major component in well being. It can be chemical, emotional or physical. The best way to visualize stress is to think of an iceberg. What we see on the surface is only a small part of the picture. We carry stress in our daily lives from events past. It's like we're climbing a mountain with a fifty pound weight on our shoulders. Why not let go of this weight? Why keep carrying it? I make an analogy to a "stress bank." All of our stress history adds up to bad checks deposited into our stress account. When we carry these deposits, we already have a weight on us when we wake up in the morning. We are overdrawn before the day even begins. Improving our stress levels by eating, thinking and feeling better is essential to our growth. Identify which foods you are sensitive to and what your needs are, and what works for you, and what doesn't. For example: your ideal sleeping hours or the latest time you should have dinner.

By depositing good checks into our stress account we will ease the weight on our shoulders so that our climb on the mountain of life will be much easier. Waking up with zero in our account is better than having an overdraft. Eventually we build up equity that will enable us to stay strong in times of stress. With bad deposits, even small stressors can wear us out. Reducing negative stress factors is our ultimate priority. Aspire to eliminate, or at least reduce, anything that doesn't nurture you. This can be applied to our relationships, friends or our work situation. We deserve to have healthy stress equity. By changing our stress patterns we change our resonance with the Universe. These changes can include being with people who do or do not enhance us, getting more or less exercise and doing too much or not enough contemplation. In short, knowing what feeds us as opposed to what doesn't.

Stress can manifest itself in any part of our body. In Astrology, each Zodiac sign has a particular body part associated with it. The assignment of the first Zodiac symbol starts at the head and ends with the feet where the last symbol is located. For example, those of us who are born under the sign of Aries would pay attention to possible health sensitivity in their head, and those who are born under Pisces would pay attention to their feet.

Sign	Dates	Body Part
Aries	March 21 - April 20	Head
Taurus	April 21 - May 21	Neck
Gemini	May 22 - June 21	Shoulders
Cancer	June 22 - July 22	Chest
Leo	July 23 -August 21	Heart
Virgo	August 22 - September 23	Abdomen
Libra	September 24 - October 23	Waist

20

Scorpio	October 24 - November 22	Genitals
Sagittarius	November 23 - December 22	Hips
Capricorn	December 23 - January 20	Knees
Aquarius	January 21 - February 19	Calves
Pisces	February 20- March 20	Feet

The organ or body part assigned to our sign is also a key to understanding some of our core lessons. For a Scorpio, the genitals, their lesson will follow the theme of fertility, creativity and sexuality and for a Capricorn the knees represent their flexibility.

Use Numerology to Find Core Issues

Another powerful way to connect with our particular issues would be through Numerology. Find your Core Number by adding up all the digits in your birth date. Then take the resulting 2 digit numbers and add them together. Example: June 29, 1961 = 6/29/1961 = 6+2+9+1+9+6+1 = 34. 3+4=7. The core number in this example is 7.

This number represents some strengths and core issues in your life. The system of Numerology is very revealing in understanding the correlation between the Universe and our lives. Once you have found what your core number is, take a look at the symbolic meaning of core numbers on the Numerology Chart in Appendix VI.

Now let's take a close look at the transformation process. As we work on different organs through the feet, we open up energy lines and increase circulation to the respective organs. The change we are allowing to take place travels through our emotional body, for this is the realm of ultimate resistance and healing. So, every point on the foot has some emotional correspondence to it. Most of these points represent some form of fear.

**Fear is an inherent emotion and releasing it
is the most important part of healing.**

Take time to reflect and journal on the various aspects of fear in your life.

Chapter Four:
Our Ego and Emotions

The Enemies Within; Ego and Fear

Fear is ego's best ally. Fear is an ambassador from the kingdom of the ego and its true mission takes great diplomatic skill: Its job is to conceal love in all its forms from our consciousness. Moreover, fear is a troublesome ambassador, for the kingdom of the ego only exists as much as we allow it to. Fear's biggest concern is to lose its job as the saboteur of love. Fear exists as a contingency and its mission is extended by our ongoing endorsement.

Years ago I was living in a Southern Florida town. I met many people that seemed to be lost, drifters and hustlers who did not seem to care about their struggle. One night I dreamed that there was a flock of sheep grazing by a fenced hillside with a cliff beyond it. Just next to the sheep was a hole in the fence that leads directly to the cliff. Every once in a while a sheep would walk too close to the edge and end up falling off the cliff. I approached the shepherd and asked him to fix the fence. To my surprise, he replied "Well, if I did fix the fence, as you suggest, the sheep wouldn't hold the option of falling." It's all about making a choice.

Therefore, those who fall choose to do so. In other words, the hole in the fence is "a hole of Choice." In a perfect world with no "holes in the fence" it would be hard to make choices. Given the deep symbolism in this dream, it is possible that the shepherd stands for "god" and the sheep are the people. We all live with symbolic fences surrounding us. Some protect us, some confine us. If courage is the antidote of fear then we need to veer at times beyond the fence into the unknown in order to grow past our limitations. Fear keeps us within the boundaries, but courage allows us to move forward. Courage entails stepping into the unknown. It may cause a temporary sensation of death, as if our old self died. In this transient void, there are no guarantees as we defy fear and ego. Cultivating a courageous life is not a black and white proposition. We wonder: what truly happened to the sheep that fell off the cliff? We may never know for sure, but it is this unknowing that allows us to dwell on the edge with a certain sense of comfort. It's a gradual evolution of allowing ourselves to live on the edge where we can feel unprecedented renewal and growth.

We see that there is a connection between ego and fear and that density is a manifestation of ego. It is safe to say that with less density in our system, more love can flow in. Mental work alone cannot lessen our density. Balanced diet, detoxification, exercise, stress reduction, to name a few, will assist the body's ability to reduce its density. In all this, we witness a shift from fear to love.

Love is the antidote for fear.

Love is the ambassador of the divine kingdom (the higher power). Its mandate is eternal and it cannot be truly sabotaged. Yet, we can put it on hold by identifying with ego and fear.

24

Nevertheless, with faith, intention and healing work we can bring more love to our life as we release our density. This allows universal love to flow in to our lives.

Grief, Joy and Friends – The Emotional Spectrum

One of the key points in the body is the heart reflex in the foot. The reflex to the heart lies under the big toe. This toe is on the same energy line as the heart. Just next to the heart lie the lungs. Our lungs represent the ability of Spirit to get in touch with us. The Latin derived English word respire (or respiration) means "to reconnect with Spirit."

The lungs have a special connection to the kidneys according to Traditional Chinese Medicine (TCM). In TCM, the kidneys disperse the energy that the lungs bring in (Air). However, this flow can be interrupted by fear. The more fear we carry (kidney), the less efficient our breathing becomes. Thus, energetically, the kidneys will be less functional under fear; therefore they will disperse the Air energy less effectively. Also, the presence of fear is an indication of ego. So, the less we live in fear / ego, the more chance our Spirit gets to emerge.

It is interesting to note that the adrenal glands lay just above the kidneys. The adrenals represent courage - and courage manages fear. Courage is the antidote for fear. The Latin language is inspiring with its wisdom: Ad Renal means "above the kidneys" – courage is above fear! The kidneys represent emotional processing of fear, as much as the Adrenals represent emotional courage.

Consequently, our goal is to convert fear into courage. This is done by being aware of the dynamics of fear as a dominant emotion. Every time you feel fear, try to observe the underlying emotion. Fear never shows up alone for dinner. It likes to take willing companions with it. You may know some of fear's friends by name: Anger, Guilt, Pride and Resentment - to name a few. Most of these negative emotions are found in the abdomen and the arch of the foot. We can safely say that many negative emotions stem from fear of having vs. not having, being vs. not being.

Chapter Five:
Reflexology and Foot Reading

Classical Signs in Foot Reading

The purpose of foot reading is to observe our feet in order to understand the logic behind how our bodies are reflected in our feet. The more intense the symptom is in the foot the more acute the situation may be in the body. An acute situation can be marked by color, temperature and skin texture and deformation. For example, redness accompanied with warmth in a certain area on the foot may reflect an inflammation in the corresponding part of the body. You can find the Foot Observation Chart in Appendix VII.

Foot Observations

The toes always give a good picture of what is going on with us. This is because the toes connect to the Air element and the Air is very in tune with what's happening with our bodies. In foot reading we can see all deficiencies and excesses manifested in our feet and thus in our system. When one element overpowers another element, it is a definite sign of imbalance in our lives. Often an element will wander into another one manifested by one toe overlapping another. For example, the Fire element moves to the Air by the second toe overlapping the first toe. If Fire represents action and Air represents thinking, then this would represent actions interfering with thinking; someone who does first and thinks later. If the first toe overlaps the second, then there might be too much thinking and not enough action. There are many examples of how elements invade each other, but the bottom line is that thinking, action, feeling and survival have to be in balance with each other.

Once an imbalance or deformity is present in the toes, it will compromise energy flow. It is like we made a cut on the antennas. The 1st toe represents the head and our thinking. Toes #2 and #3 represent our eyes through which we "see" and toes #4 and #5 represent our ears through which we "hear." Any changes in our toes would reflect changes in our thinking, hearing and seeing.

Another division of the toes corresponds to The Four Elements:

AIR	TOE 1 – Big Toe
FIRE	TOE 2 – Index Toe
NEUTRAL	TOE 3 – Middle Toe
WATER	TOE 4 – Ring Toe
EARTH	TOE 5 – Pinky Toe

There exists a subdivision for each toe as well. Each toe contains all four elements. If we roughly divide each toe into 4 sections: Earth is at the base of the toe, Water is the second quarter of the toe, Fire is the third quarter of the toe and Air is the tip of the toe. If, for example, we see that Toe 4, which represents Water / emotions, has a bump on its lower mid-section, we can conclude that the emotions are especially impacted. Actually, in this case, we have a double impact: not only the specific toe that represents emotions is affected, but the section of the toe representing emotions is affected.

The Water area stretches from the diaphragm line (lowest line on Fire) to the heel line (highest line on Earth). The lower we descend on the Water area, the deeper the emotional element becomes. Any emotion that is NOT processed may end up "on the bottom of the lake." It is really like a ship that sinks in water – there is only so far it can go until it hits the sand on the bottom.

The abdominal floor is like the bottom of the lake.
It is to where unprocessed emotions sink.

Thus, any attempt to stir up this area may result in the release of potential unprocessed stuff. Often, like with any release but even more pronounced, this will manifest as excessive dreaming of all sorts and even actual excessive bowel movements. These bowel movements will be foul in nature due to the highly toxic contents.

When the Water-Earth area is congested, one may feel trapped and lack in life flow. This can sometimes result in feelings of terror. Having many unprocessed emotions "stuck" in our Water-Earth border may lead to an inability to do deep processing of subsequent events which translates into a feeling of terror – severe fear with no escape. As this area is opened up and thus made less dense, we feel free and receptive to new experiences, free of fear and anxiety.

There exists a polar connection between the feet and the head. Just like the feet represent the world of "matter" or "the world of forms" with its burdens and limitations, so does the head represent the world of "energy" or the "world of non-forms." This polarity creates a balance – we do not aspire to live only "in here" or only "out there." We aspire to find a balance between our physical reality and our energetic existence, our higher self. Connecting with the higher self is in our best interest - as it will lead to rejuvenation. Our master glands, pituitary and hypothalamus, are in the head. As we balance our polarities through conscious intention and body work, we are likely to surrender and reconcile the polarity between our physical reality and that of our higher self.

"Brian" is a 37 year old musician who likes to work hard and play harder. He is tall, slender and very strong. He owns his own landscaping business and works six days a week, but always makes time to party when he can. During an initial foot reading I conducted with him, his big toe was lifted upward in a position indicating an arrogant self perception. He reported the general sensation of stagnation in his life and came to me for some guidance. My initial thoughts were that he was disconnected from himself and acted on old patterns that no longer served him well such as a poor relationship with his parents or a sense of isolation. By the end of the sessions he was moving to a better place, interested in staying healthy and reported a higher satisfaction of living. His primary goal was to have more energy and better vitality. Through our work on his endocrine system and the second toe, which represents habits and the connection to the heart, he made physiological and dispositional improvements.

Let's take another look at the statement "As above, so below." These are parallel opposites; since "below" is our actual world of matter, our feet, then 'above' is represented by our heads. When density is released in our feet it opens up our head, therefore inviting more serenity and clarity. So the more we open up our soles the more in touch we become with our souls. It could be beneficial to go through foot reflexology sessions in order to truly experience this, however understanding these principles in themselves will allow for much change and growth. Removing the density of the feet (the "below") is crucial to our emotional/mental/spiritual growth (the "above"). It is an organic approach to therapy where we don't just talk out our problems, but we approach them where they may truly exist - at the "stitch" between our body and soul.

Chapter Six:
Release and Renewal

Balancing Our Surroundings

All of our body systems act in perfect harmony with their intended functions. The basic rule for health is balance and reconciliation of opposites. Beyond the polarities (e.g. sun vs. moon, masculine vs. feminine) there is the notion that in order to attain balance between poles, we must first understand and know each of them separately. Only then can we find the balance between them. For example, female reproductive issues are an expression of imbalances of femininity, receptivity and fertility. It's essential to reach a point where one acquaints oneself with the masculine / feminine dichotomy, in this case Fire vs. Water. When both Fire and Water are better understood, balance is created.

**In order to be complete and balanced, we
must embrace the principles of our own gender
while being mindful of those of the opposite gender.**

If action is a masculine principle, then reflection is feminine. In every human being there is both a feminine and a masculine psychological element and we all need to be aware and develop these polar aspects to their fullest manifestation. We always want to start by identifying first with our own gender then explore the other gender as it manifests itself in our psyche. Ultimately every action, thought or feeling can be seen within the range of our own balance, as true oneness is both male and female.

On the physical level it is important to clean up any clutter in your house to achieve a balance. Throw away whatever doesn't serve you anymore and open your "closets" to new possibilities. If you haven't worn an item for 12 months you may not need it. Give it away. By letting go we invite in the new. The same goes for our refrigerator and cupboards. Look for any food that went bad or expired and throw it away. The food in our house corresponds to how we nurture ourselves. By keeping only good and healthy foods we tell the Universe that we are happily and responsibly nurturing ourselves.

In Chinese philosophy Chi energy is the life force. Chi represents the flow of life force. Have you ever entered a room and felt either uplifted or drained? You probably responded to the life force present in that space. We want our own space to reflect a good flow of Chi. Monitor the colors you surround yourself with and see how harmonious they are with you and those with whom you live. Keep a live plant in every room, if possible. Use candles or sage smudge, which represent the Fire element, to clean the air of its impurities. In general, look around your living space and reflect on how your choices of objects represent who you are right now. Add an item that represents who you want to become. Look at your choice of music that you like and ask yourself why you like it.

Look at music you don't like and ask yourself the same question. Overall, see how the choices you make on a daily basis e.g. clothing, eating and talking reflect the harmonious life which is your birthright.

Balancing Our pH

Factors in our health, such as our pH, can change. I studied urine and saliva pH analysis where we determined how our pH is an indicator of how we live our life. When there was a big gap between the urine and saliva pH (over 2 points) it was an indication that our actual life is stressed out: there was a large gap between our actual life and the life we were meant to live. By connecting better with our higher self and eliminating stress factors our urine and saliva pH levels eventually become equal or close to each other. When we harmonize our life - people, places and circumstances all change around us. We will meet new people, somewhat different from before. People will bring us deeper messages as we resonate better with their frequencies. We find ourselves in better and new places as the circumstances of our life also change. An important way to balance our pH is to harmonize our diet, drink alkalizing water (see lemon water below) and reduce / eliminate acidic foods and beverages such as alcohol, coffee, sugar and meat.

When through specific dietary changes we alkalize our pH and de-acidify our tissues we consequently get less dense. Some people find water mixed with lemon juice helpful in this alkalizing process. This connection between mind and body is reciprocal. They both affect each other. A very important factor that is sometimes overlooked in the search for well being is how well we absorb nutrients and how balanced our body's pH is. Taking a look at body pH, we can see that. In general, acidity always equals toxicity. Ideally we will have a balanced pH by reducing acidic foods such as meat, soda, dairy, and sugar, as well as bad water (acidic, chlorinated, toxic, etc.).

Acid and alkaline also correspond to our thoughts and aspirations.

For example, aggressive thoughts and victim-consciousness cause our system to be more acidic. The balance of acid and alkaline corresponds to the balance of negative and positive, Yin and Yang. Thoughts of love and appreciation can be alkalizing in that they bring us back to balance. Conscious breathing is alkalizing. Most of us tend to be acidic, usually in our urine and blood more than our saliva. Our pH is a major component of the mechanism of homeostasis. Homeostasis is the stability of the inner environment in the body. It is greatly affected by the sum of all our stress factors, our DNA and our experiences. I often see people who have parents or siblings with Diabetes. They themselves may carry the predisposition for Diabetes, but usually it takes a very stressful event to trigger the onset of the condition. We can say that our overall strength is as strong as the weakest link in our DNA chain. Striving to maintain a balanced life on all levels will greatly reduce the chance of breaking the weakest link in our chain.

Proper exercise that reduces stress, maintains flexibility and muscle tone is highly beneficial to life balance. Bodywork is also highly recommended. I have found Yoga, especially Phoenix Rising Yoga Therapy to be of benefit. I had an injury in my T6 vertebrae, right in the middle of my ribcage, which made it painful for me to breath. After working with Phoenix Rising therapy the pain intensified for two weeks, then once while I was lying in bed I noticed that my breathing was much deeper. Consequently my back pain disappeared. The therapist worked on my back by using all kinds of manipulations, yet she also detected that these blockages may have had to do with a childhood event of some sort.

It just felt wonderful to breathe deeply once again. See more about Foods to Change to Balance Our pH in Appendix VIII.

Balancing Our Sugar

A great analogy to understand the power of life is to take a look at love. Love is the ultimate power! Loving ourselves and others empowers us. It is only by love that we draw on the interconnectedness of all humans. In our daily experience the physical equivalent for how we circulate love in our life is sugar. The better we circulate sugar in our bodies the more likely we are to give and take love freely. Sugar also represents self-realization. When our sugar is balanced we tend to be more self realized, meaning that we are living the life we are meant to live. Low or high blood sugar, as well as sugar abuse, is a sign of possible love issues. Note that many people go on a sugar binge when they are frustrated. Sugar releases serotonin in the brain and gives a sense of happiness and contentment.

A more elaborate form of sugar is alcohol. Here we have fermented sugar, and if sugar represents love then alcohol represents fermented love. One of the main principles of the AA program is to re-establish a connection with the higher power and eliminate the faulty perception that one is isolated and alone. Fermented sugar is fermented love and consuming it is an attempt to connect with love, but just like fermentation means something is stale, consuming alcohol means consuming stale love – a love that is isolated, not flowing and disconnected. It may be true that alcohol can give a temporary release and relief, but one always goes back to the same place of isolation. The only way to connect with true self love is by true work. Staleness is the opposite of flow and only that which flows is true. There is nothing wrong with consuming alcohol, but alcohol abuse is a cry for help to improve the flow of love in one's life. By drinking excessively, one unknowingly admits being stale when it comes to self love and love in general. The only people who can give love are those who are able to accept love.

Life is meant to be sweet. When you remind yourself of the sweet moments in your life your consciousness grows where your attention goes. When we lose the sense of sweetness we may become bitter and frustrated. Frustration is a disconnection between our soul and energy self and our body or our physical self. When we are frustrated our energy is frustrated because we are not letting it manifest in our real physical life. Love is the antidote to frustration and with it comes self acceptance and love for others. The opposite of frustration is self-realization. When we feel realized we are comfortable here and now.

In fact, no matter what our circumstances are, we want to feel good right now. It is this feeling good right now that allows our balance to flow. The ego would want to jump in and say something like "yes, but how can I feel good now when this is happening - I have debt, I am ill, the world is in crisis". Nevertheless healing starts from within and healing starts in this moment. To feel good now, just pause and say, "I choose to feel good now." Now watch your breathing, and if it is not deep, take a big breath and say it again. Some theories about breathing go as far as speculating that the body's pH can change with better breathing. What can be better proof of the mind-body connection than the importance of breathing? What we feel now determines how our present unfolds. Let's choose to feel good now. And so it is.

Almost all illness stems from frustration, resistance and misunderstanding. When we allow ourselves to deserve and accept unconditional love and when we free ourselves of fear, guilt and shame by forgiving ourselves and others, we remove the emotional stumbling blocks that deny our right to be happily present. This doesn't mean that everything will be just perfect in our life. It just means that we claim our divine right to be happy and self fulfilled and we open up to the infinite possibilities that the Universe has in store for us.

The Universe is a good listener:
whatever we tell it will be amplified.

Be very mindful of what you truly tell the Universe. It is
okay to have fears and doubts, yet it is very important to aspire to
live beyond them or else we just keep living through them. See that
all suffering is based on misunderstanding. Even the worst events
are based in our perceptions and what we make of them right at
this moment. It is not so much about what happens to us as much
as what we make out of it. At this very moment, choose to be free
of the shackles of the past. The past is past and we grow only from
good and fulfilling perceptions of it, a fuel for our wonderful future
experiences. All is well.

Every time we move forward it entails some sacrifice of the
"I" which means some death of the ego. Only when we learn to
gradually replace our ego-based perceptions with higher self-
perceptions, do we open ourselves to be a part of the whole and
also take responsibility for the whole. Healing is gradually
removing the ego layer which is standing between us and our
higher self. The "I" that we identify with can hardly ever be saved
or enlightened. It is like taking a blind friend to a silent movie. It is
the known "I" or the higher self, that gradually evolves through
knowing. The higher self can never be attacked by others. The
higher self has a sense of boundary, but at the same time
interconnectedness. Its sense of boundary is only that it is not
engaging in other people's ego gains, but it always responds
favorably to others' higher self.

Withholding love is one of the common ailments of the "I"
since many of us feel that we didn't receive enough love ourselves.
Love transcends all barriers and opposites and is the ultimate
union. It is timeless and therefore has no fear of death. Love is the
eternal truth of interconnectedness. It is often challenged in our

daily activities, but keeping a deep sense of love can shape all of our daily experiences to the miraculous extent of completely shifting our encounters, the contents and the outcomes: people, places and circumstances.

Many resources are utilized in the research for one of man's most powerful illnesses, cancer. We have invested great effort in research yet the success is still limited. Cancer is in essence similar to love in that cancer spreads and tries to unite all the cells of different tissues and thus becomes all encompassing. It is when we withhold love that disease can take hold of us. Cancer imitates the modus operandi of true love by becoming all encompassing. Just like love, cancer aspires to extend to everything. Just like love, cancer has no fear. Cancer resembles true love that is not allowed to be expressed. It's like a deep secret that can't be shared. The answer to cancer, or at least one important answer to cancer, is seeing it as a symptom of misplaced love. Opening the heart to unconditional love that defies hurt could be helpful to understanding cancer.

Unconditional love resides in the heart Chakra and corresponds to the heart. It is very interesting that the heart is the only organ that does not contract cancer. The heart can "break," as in a heart attack, but can never contract cancer. Consequently, it is the message of the heart that unconditional love can defy almost anything. This includes the need to manifest unexpressed love on the wrong level just like in the case of cancer. Like with many illnesses, the answer lies with looking within us and at how we circulate the ultimate power of the Universe, love. The root of suffering is the perception of the self as existing separately. In accepting interconnectedness and love as the only true powers in life, the ego automatically allows for the higher self or the true self to govern our daily activities. Only then can we manifest better health for us and others.

Understanding Stress

Stress is the one ultimate factor that affects our well being. Stress is a condition which affects organs as a result of repetitive stressful conditions. There are many factors in stress: physical, mental and emotional. On the physical level, the air we breathe, the exercise we get and the quality of food and water we eat and drink (e.g. additives, coloring, preservatives, pollution, heavy metal and metabolic waste) affect our stress levels. On the mental and emotional levels our thoughts, fears, core beliefs and self esteem are all stress factors.

The Nervous System

The physical body governs stress through the nervous system, which has three parts:
1. Central Nervous System – the brain and the spine. This is the place of the high command, processing information and deciding what to do with it.
2. Peripheral Nervous System – serves the central nervous system. Gathers information from the entire body and communicates to the organs. It is located throughout the body.
3. Autonomic Nervous System has two parts:
   a. Sympathetic Nervous System
This system is in charge of how the body functions under stress. It governs the Three F's: fight, fright or flight mechanism. It is in charge of preparing the body for an emergency situation through the secretion of the adrenal glands. Adrenaline secretion prepares the body to act under stress by contracting the blood vessels. This creates more blood pressure to feed nutrients to the

muscles which are expected to soon require extra help.

Imagine a rabbit that spots a fox in the field. The rabbit may automatically prepare itself for emergency action. Depending on many factors, the rabbit may decide to stay still. For example, if the wind is blowing in his favor he might decide not to risk himself by moving and disclose its location. Still--if we take a close look at the rabbit--it is shivering although it is not really moving. This is because the rabbit is actually preparing itself through the Sympathetic Nervous System for movement, although it is hasn't necessarily elected to move yet. With the slightest scare, the rabbit is ready to jump.

In this situation, the body is prepared for action regardless of the ultimate choice. In humans, this stressful preparation for action can happen even under a perceived threat. Fear and worry can activate the Sympathetic Nervous System causing hypertension because blood pressure needs to rise to prepare the body for perceived action. Often the body has little to no time to clear itself of the overload of adrenaline that flows through it. The automatic secretion of adrenaline under stress can sometimes be toxic.

b. Parasympathetic Nervous System (PNS)

This system serves as a counterbalance for the Sympathetic Nervous System. The PNS is in charge of relaxing and restoring balance once the Sympathetic Nervous System has run its course. For example, after the rabbit is out of danger, the adrenaline secretion diminishes and the Parasympathetic System kicks-in in order to restore normalcy. However, when our lives are under too much stress the body seems to fall into a sympathetic or hypertensive rut where it never truly restores a state of balance. Therefore, a body in this state stays under the spell of the Sympathetic Nervous System.

Breathing

Breathing is a very important process of exchanging gasses, absorption of oxygen and release of CO2. Oxygen is considered alkalizing and CO2 is acidifying. A healthy state of homeostasis is created by keeping the balance between alkaline and acidity. This balance between oxygen and CO2 is a part of homeostasis. The respiratory system acquires blockages easily. It's a very muscular area, including the diaphragm and the inter-costal muscles of the chest. Every time we get scared, worried or panicked, we may stop breathing for a moment and as a pattern this may create blockages in the breathing system. It could result in shallow breathing. Shallow breathers are usually less present. Deep breathers are usually more present.

**Improving our breathing
is a basic step in improving
our awareness of the here and now.**

There are many causes that stop the breathing. Some are fear, anger or hatred. As we stop breathing we stop the flow of life. Of course, we don't stop breathing completely, but even a partial breath can set in the muscles to create blockages that affect our body and our life. As our breathing is compromised, we absorb less oxygen which can cause us to be more acidic. We can become more nervous and tired. Yawning is usually an attempt to restore this lack of oxygen. A physical blockage that causes contraction of the muscles in the chest area is also energetic as it creates a situation where we do not allow our Fire element to come to action. Since our lungs represent our ability to inhale life and exhale loss, any lung problem could denote feelings of grief or depression – the feelings that we don't deserve to live a full life.

In traditional Astrology, the exact moment of our birth is determined when our first breath is taken – when our soul enters our body. Our breathing represents our relationship with our soul, but also with the world around us. This is the significance of respiration. When we breathe we are forced to exchange energy with the environment. In fact, if we had to stay in a room with a person we did not like we might not talk to each other, yet we still have to breathe the same air. Breathing therefore represents the ultimate interconnectedness because we all share the same air. We can go without food for several weeks and without water for several days, but it takes only several minutes to expire from suffocation. This exemplifies how air is an essential element on the physical level.

Breathing also represents the process of exchange - giving and taking. In this paradigm, just like air is available to us, and Air element represents the infinite, any lack that we may have in our lives is there because we have cut ourselves off from the infinite. Breathing is also the ultimate mode of being present. When you have breathing problems, ask yourself what it is that you don't relate to in the present moment. With an infinite supply of air we should be breathing smoothly. Having breathing problems can signify that we are cut off from our souls or essence, and we refuse to be present.

> **"In breathing there are two blessings**
> **Drawing breath, releasing it again,**
> **The one pressurizes us, the other refreshes us,**
> **So wonderfully blended is life."**
> **- Johann Wolfgang von Goethe**
>
> —

It is interesting to note how the breathing process is affected by our story. Many children came from homes where they didn't feel safe whether from an alcoholic parent or violence. Since a five-year-old can't really run away, the child often disconnects himself from the environment by cutting off breath flow. By breathing more shallowly, the child is attempting to create boundaries with the environment and the air that we all breathe. Since children cannot normally escape their situation, their only means of escape may be to create a false boundary by refusing to breathe smoothly. In fact, breathing shallowly can be a sign of disconnecting and disassociating. Notice your breath in times of stress and fear. We often don't breathe well under these circumstances. It is like we try to disconnect from that which threatens us by severing our breathing process. Therefore, breathing is the ultimate gauge for being present. How could a child who felt threatened constantly want to breathe smoothly? It is only natural for a child to want to sever his breathing under certain circumstances.

As a pattern, shallow breathing can be damaging because it draws on the old paradigm that the world is unsafe. It is important, through yoga and breathing exercises, to improve breathing as it is our best ticket for the here and now. Breathing represents giving and taking and in a threatening environment there's only so much we can take. One of the most common core beliefs is that the world is unsafe and hostile. Severing our breathing is one of our first strategies to try and establish boundaries between us and our environment.

There are other connections to the breathing process - the lungs connect with the emotion of grief and the colon connects with the emotion of forgiveness. Shallow breathing and constipation go hand-in-hand. When a child doesn't want to exchange energy with the world, constipation is the child's version of not participating. Constipation draws often on an old pattern stemming from childhood of refusing to partake or participate in the family life. A child who is refusing to give and take because of a perception of the world as being hostile often responds in shallow breathing and constipation when growing into adulthood.

Breathing is also a rhythmic activity. Rhythm is one of the

secrets of life. If we look at breathing closely, we may reveal some of the deeper meanings of life as well. We take in air, expand and then we release and thus contract. It is between this expansion and contraction that all life prevails. Breathing in corresponds to "all" and breathing out corresponds to nothingness. In a good and balanced sense of self, we remember that on the one hand the whole world is created just for us and yet, on the other hand we are nothing, dust of the Earth. Remembering that we exist in between the polarity of wholeness and nothingness will allow a healthier and balanced sense of self.

The secret lies in the ability to relate to both truths at the same time. This draws on the breathing process of all versus nothing. In other words, by contemplating breathing we draw on important principles that relate to our lives. The healing abilities of the body are infinite. Simply look at the power of the placebo effect to find a convincing argument for the healing powers of the mind. There is a famous case of a teenage girl who had Lupus disease for which she was taking medicine. The pills she took were causing strong side effects, so her doctors decided to give her pills made of chalk which looked identical to the ones she had before. Surprisingly, the girl remained symptom free despite no longer taking the actual medication. Unfortunately, there is not much money to be made in placebo medicine and it doesn't always work. However, it seems important to research the placebo response because study groups given the placebo thinking they are taking the actual medication have often showed marked improvement.

A very interesting approach to natural healing is demonstrated by Dr. Edward Bach who researched the connection between emotions to nature. In his view, disease is a message to change and an opportunity to be aware of our shortcomings. In 1930 Dr. Bach left a successful homeopathic practice in London to go to the countryside and develop a new line of natural medicines made from wild flowers. He meticulously observed the connection between nature and human suffering until he was able to correlate different plants with different human emotional conditions. He acknowledged that the emotions of a child are very important in his or her evolution. Primarily, he discovered the Holly flower as the ultimate heart opener for unresolved childhood emotions (for example: hate, jealousy and fear). It is interesting that Holly branches became an important symbol of Christmas, the holiday of unconditional love. Holly flowers, according to Dr. Bach, represent unconditional love that defies anger and jealousy.

**The emotions of anger, jealousy and withholding love crystallize in childhood and
– unless addressed –
may remain present for the rest of our lives.**

Our Filtration System

There exists a connection between the lungs and the kidneys. In Traditional Chinese Medicine (TCM) both of these organs take charge of the respiration system. With ongoing breathing impairments, caused by the presence of fear, we can also create a blockage in the kidneys. In TCM the kidney is the seat of the Jing which is a life energy that we are born with and is connected to the essence of life. The idea is that we are all born with our personal dose of Jing and the secret is to disperse this energy wisely throughout our lives by living a balanced lifestyle - or else we can get burnt out. When we are breathing oxygen, the kidneys collect their energy and then disperse it into the body. Therefore, in TCM the energy from breathing is dispersed through the kidneys. The lungs handle the mechanical part of the breathing process whereas the kidneys handle the energetic part. It is safe to say that in TCM the kidneys are a part of the respiratory system, among other systems.

The kidneys filter the blood. Blood represents joy. The

kidneys have the ability to filtrate our emotional experiences. The more flowing the kidneys, the better we process our emotional experiences. Fear ties to the kidneys and with the presence of fear kidney function can be reduced. This often results in a decreased ability to process our emotions and therefore allowing more fear to set in. When the kidneys are affected, people tend to dwell on past experiences of fear and will process present events from the perspective of these past experiences. For example, a woman who has experienced rape may be unable to enjoy dating as she could dwell on the past trauma. Consequently, an impaired kidney cannot filter the blood well and, since blood represents joy, it would be very difficult to keep joy in our system. *Fear kills joy.* Interestingly, the kidneys are also connected to the knees. Have you ever had your knees shivering in a state of extreme fear? The knees represent our ego and our ability to bend over and be flexible. Since the kidneys represent fear and fear governs ego, consequently there is a connection between the kidneys and the knees.

The kidneys are a Water element and in reflexology they are located in the Water area of the foot. They also balance the body's fluids. A weak kidney can cause edema or water retention. Kidneys also balance sodium and phosphate in the body which balances the body's pH levels. Mentally, the kidney's filtration denotes the ability to determine what is important and what is not. It is the ability to release what does not serve us so to only keep the lessons that best serve us. With healthy kidney function even in an unpleasant situation we should still be able to filter the events of the present moment.

A good kidney doesn't flush away the "good" or the "bad" in our bodies. It processes everything, without judgment, and keeps the important message. It is important to be able to see and feel everything prior to releasing the physical/emotional debris. The eyes also connect to the kidneys. Fear impairs our ability to see forward and often people with kidney conditions can have eye issues. Kidneys also filter emotions of morality and regret. Unscrupulous actions may also affect kidney function as the kidneys represent a universal sense of discernment. Remember that kidneys filter blood and blood circulation corresponds to how we circulate joy in our life.

Psycho-neuro-immunology – The Mind-Body Connection

Some body organs give us a clue about the connection between the body and the energetic fields that surround us. The thymus is an organ that connects our mental / emotional body or the psyche through the nervous system and our immune system (hence psycho-neuro-immunology). Located within the heart Chakra of unconditional love the thymus is the organ that reflects harmony. Well being is ultimately contingent on the strength of the immune system and the immune system responds to our thoughts and feelings as transmitted through the nervous system. In other words, there exists a connection between health and thoughts, between well being and feeling. Psycho-neuro-immunology (PNI) refers to the ability of the mind to alter the function of our immune system which is responsible for defying disease.

Nowhere in recorded history was the thymus as important as in the 1980's with the appearance of AIDS. The thymus produces T cells that are vital to immune function. Under stress the thymus' ability to produce T cells is compromised. Until the AIDS epidemic, many medical schools thought that the thymus' importance decreased after puberty. It was thought that it is important until puberty and then it shrinks from the size of a fist to a walnut. It is ironic that it took the outbreak of AIDS to make us realize we still don't know everything about health and that T cell production is crucial to the rest of our lives beyond puberty. As an organ that sits in the center of the Psycho-neuro-immunology system, the thymus is a key T cell producer and, therefore, the immune system's gate keeper.

**When we reduce overall stress we improve immunity.
Stress is the sum of the manner in which we
live, eat, work, think and feel.**

When we change our thoughts we improve our reality, as
our reality is a projection of our thoughts which are a result of our
inner flow. There is an observation that everything that happens on
Earth is synonymous with higher processes and that AIDS reflects
a universal immunity crisis due to global warming, pollution and
overpopulation. The Earth's own immunity became compromised.
The message inherent in the thymus is harmony and rhythm. When
the body or the world for that matter is out of harmony, a distortion
in the immunity occurs. We are all told to develop a balanced
lifestyle. Perhaps global warming is an indication of immune
deficiency in the world, and therefore a lack of balance and
harmony. We are drawn more and more into the collective aspect
of life where separation becomes less and less possible. If personal
immune issues remain personal and affect a specific person then
global immune issues go beyond singular suffering and thus
become all encompassing.

We are also told to lead a pro-active and more holistic life
where we can't afford to only focus on our own backyard. Green
issues such as toxic fuel emissions, heavy metals in ocean water
and contamination in food create a more immediate ecological and
energetic impact on our lives. It all comes full circle. Fortunately,
we possess the key for a possible reversal of fortunes in that energy
has always superseded matter. Therefore, with a new thought and
belief system, harnessed into taking action, physical reality can
shift. Having more thoughts and acts of compassion and unity
would create a higher frequency of universal resonance.

We already know that every thought we think exists in
reality and affects us and our surroundings. It is never too late to

change thought patterns. We are entering a time of increasing challenge. With this, resistance to change keeps inflicting more suffering. It is important to identify ego patterns of fear and resistance to change and allow for a higher reality to emerge. Change is in fact possible. Unfortunately, no other force can instigate change as much as suffering. Suffering is a modus operandi of the ego and often it is disguised under a fun-seeking lifestyle. Having fun is great, yet identifying patterns that lead to suffering is as important. We can only change the world one thing at a time and one kind action at a time. We need to focus on our passion and see how through it we are capable of a connection to the greater good.

Random acts of kindness can be just that, random. What is even more powerful is when our acts of kindness are funneled through our areas of passion and joy, those that reflect our character. For example, if you are an animal lover you can extend your kind actions through your love of animals. If you are a natural healer realize how your small daily interactions make a difference in other people's lives. Know who you are and harness that knowledge for the greater good. It will all come back to you as a stronger energy and purpose in your own life. Tying ourselves to the greater good is a win-win situation. Energetically speaking, it is like the power of light. *The more light that we share, the more light we can draw from the Universe to ourselves.* What we reap is what we sow and what we focus on grows and manifests.

The thymus is a reminder, through its vicinity to the heart, that this area of the body is the true core - just like in the romance languages the word for heart and center are the same. Another important message from the thymus and heart area is to live a heart centered life. Every thought, decision and action should be heart-centered. Meaning that it is necessary to be aligned with the heart center before it is manifested. There is a powerful exercise to improve heart centered living. When you talk with another person, send a beam of light from the middle of your forehead to their forehead. At the same time send another beam from your heart to the same point in the other person's forehead. As you are doing this you will gradually align the projections of your thoughts with your heart vibration. Only that which is heart-based will be communicated.

Most people talk from forehead-to-forehead, therefore from mind to mind, speaking only from logic and ego. Ultimately we would communicate only from heart to heart, but to reach this point it's beneficial to combine heart and head first. Speaking and acting heart-to-heart is challenging because it draws on the fourth Chakra essence of unconditional love. You can try and exercise heart-to-heart communication. If it proves difficult, just try it again another time. Remember the middle phase is to engage your mind and heart while thinking and communicating with another person's mind and heart.

Do not confuse the mind with the brain. When we talk about "mind" we relate to the self with its identifications and not the brain itself. If we recognize the human being as more than a mechanism to be repaired when it malfunctions we already acknowledge a dialogue between different aspects of existence as opposed to an isolated separate body. In Eastern teachings, the concept of Chi or life force is prevailing. Chi is life force and we enhance Chi by embracing our life. By looking only at the physical aspects of the body, allopathic medicine ignores the existence of energy fields. It is somewhat like trying to understand the sounds of a radio by analyzing its parts.

One of the biggest challenges that we face
when we are changing
is to break habits
which no longer serve our highest good.

These habits are nestled deep in our core and are difficult

to get rid of. Our heart and our habits are connected through rhythm. Habits are rhythmic patterns of behavior. It is much easier to change habits in our life when we pay attention to rhythm. For example, breathing, do you breathe in rhythm? Are you capable of thinking and breathing at the same time? Do you stop breathing when you are scared? When you think of someone who hurt you does your breathing become shallow? Just as heart and rhythm are core issues in change, so is breathing. It's the ultimate connection between our souls and our life force.

It is no accident that the lungs and heart are neighbors and that they both dwell in the chest cavity, the abode of Fire. Fire represents habits and bad habits can burn us out. Harmony can only be achieved through mastering good habits. An interesting habit to be mentioned here is smoking. In smoking we put a smokescreen in the pathway of breathing, therefore, screening the connection between us and our souls. It is like dwelling on an unresolved situation and deciding not to decide. Inaction is action as well – an act of resistance. It is also a result of the pain that is inherent in facing our souls and smoke-screening is a temporary pain reliever for the soul (remember the lungs/soul connection). It is no wonder that smoking is an incredibly difficult habit to break. Habits and symptoms are alike in that they may be a sign of us being stuck in unresolved patterns. If we took a closer look into our symptoms and their meanings the answer may reveal some specific information about our own makeup.

Reflexology teaches us that the whole arch area represents the Water element which relates to our emotions. Roughly speaking, the upper Water area also represents our conscious emotions, those that we are aware of and the lower Water area represents our subconscious emotions, those that truly affect our life. In other words the lower we descend from the diaphragm (which is the Fire / Water border between the ball of the foot and the arch) the deeper and less conscious the emotional realm becomes. The next border on the abdominal area is between the

Water and Earth areas; the arch and the heel. The closer we get to this border the deeper we delve into our subconscious. When emotions that are not processed well have nowhere to go they sink down into this area and form a blockage that can create ultimate fear and terror.

We humans are microcosms and reflections of the Universe. We contain the sum total of all the aspects of being within our consciousness. Our path through the parallel worlds of energy and matter necessitates us to reconcile this polarity in our daily experience. In order to recognize the energy and matter polarity we need to first acknowledge that it exists. Often the more we identify with the physical reality the more imbalance we create on the energetic one. In some aspects, our repressed parts are consistent with the shadow, the part in us that we suppress. Manifesting symptoms of imbalance such as disease and illness can make us honest by bringing that which we have repressed to light. Think of it as work in progress. We have to aspire to see everything around us without letting our ego get involved or judge it. We have to learn to contemplate with detachment and ease of breath. It is only by attaching ourselves to a greater reality of existence that we can truly become a part of the real world.

Intention, Direction and Symbolism

To be in sync means to be open and part of the universal flow. Never doubt your intuition. Our intuition is our soul's intention and direction. In Hebrew the root word KVN is the same for intention and direction. Intention is KaVaNa and direction is KiVuN. The ultimate intention and direction is the one that is in alignment with our higher self. Any disturbance in our direction and / or intention is a sort of "blind spot" in our energy flow. This "blind spot" is a part of our density. With intention we can change direction.

On the feet there can be corns, distortions or spurs. Also, on our feet, the ultimate blockages can be found in the spine reflex which is the center of awareness and on the toes that represent our perceptions. For example vertebrae C1—the 1st Cervical Vertebrae at the top or our spine--represents how we let the entire spine awareness flow into our head. Since C1 is the link between the spine and our head, a cluster of dead skin on this spot, for example, may represent a blockage in the flow between awareness and perception. By "opening up" this point on the foot we can see more contact and connection between these two aspects.

Interestingly enough, the spine also represents nine months of pregnancy. In the Spinal Chart of the Foot in Appendix IX, C1 (which falls on the foot on the medial part of both big toes, just beside the base of the nail, it feels like a bump) also represents the time of our conception. It shows the quality of energy present from both sides (mother and father) at conception time. Any disturbance in this initial energy (for example, parents not getting along) will affect the flow between our awareness and perception. If this flow is severed we can expect the Air element, which is the toes, to show some imbalance - for example, toe nail deformation. By certain manipulation of the C1 area on the foot we can break this blockage and create more flow. This breakage may manifest itself by us feeling more aware and lucid. Our intention and direction can only be as clear as the energy flowing through us. The more openness the more flow.

"Beth", a client of mine in her early fifties, was molested by her stepfather when she was twelve. She did not have accurate memories of the events. However, as an adult she had an interesting recurring dream. In her dream she was swimming in a pool and a whale was leaping on her trying to drown her. As she was being attacked by the whale, her father watches from a corner without coming to her aid.

Beth's toes were very uneven, both in length and order. Each toe seemed to zigzag up and down, but this was much more

apparent on her right foot, the father foot. It was apparent to me
that an event had taken place that disturbed her Air element and
affected her ability to develop an even toe line. This type of trauma
can affect one on many levels. Beth never developed the "security
belt", that layer of protective fat around the belly—which signifies
a shield around the second Chakra; the sexual Chakra. However
her sister developed the protective shield around her belly. Beth
had assumed that her sister was also molested, yet never found an
appropriate occasion to ask her. Besides, her sister was much
closed regarding sexual matters, so any attempt to discuss it would
have been futile. The reason her sister had the protective layer and
Beth didn't could be that Beth was working on the issue and her
sister was negating it.

A distorted mind is fed by distorted grounding. When our
feet (the representatives of being grounded) don't serve as good
grounding tools the mind is affected. To this end any deformation
in our feet, any blockage, may be a sign of a "mis-under-standing."
It is where universal energy doesn't flow through us properly.
Opening up the blocked energy in the feet and releasing the
blockages will allow the higher powers to flow better through us
and ground our higher self in the here and now.

Sole to Soul

A polarized connection exists between the feet and the
head. Just like the feet represent this world, "the world of forms"
with its burdens and limitations, the head, "the world of energy"
represents the infinite. The polarity is such that it all conforms to
"as above, so below." The more density we release from the feet,
the more release we offer to the head. So, the more our soles are
open, the more our souls are free. Sole to Soul, that's it! In this
process of release, dreaming is very prominent. We can also
encounter more frequent bowel movements, flashbacks and deep

change. In healing work we call these "reactions."

The Kaballah mentions the density we carry as "veils." These veils are hindering cosmic light and energy from flowing through us. According to the Kaballah our bodies reflect the Divine image of God by a system of energy centers called Sephirot (note the similarity to the word spheres). These Sephirot pretty much correlate to the spheres in the Chakra system in that they are centers in the human body that reflect universal energies. Interestingly enough, the feet are related to the Sephirah (single for Sephirot) of Malkhut, a Sephirah that represents our physical world - the world of forms. This is the lowest spot in the human body and the closest to earth. This is a sphere of matter and density. Working on this center allows us to open up the density and allow lightness from the opposite pole, the head, to flow through. But it is not absolutely necessary to have reflexology treatments to benefit from this knowledge. Simply understanding these principles without having the actual physical work can prove to be very beneficial.

Understanding is a healing force in itself.

We carry our experiences in our feet. Some say we carry our experiences in every cell of the body, but ultimately, because they represent how we perceive our reality, the feet are the registrar of our experiences. Each toe represents a part of our makeup. For example, the fifth toe represents creativity and sexuality. I had a female client who wanted to have a baby very badly. Since it didn't work out (she couldn't find the right partner, timing was wrong, etc.) she manifested cysts in her uterus and ovaries. She also had benign cysts in her breasts. When I checked the small toes (the fifth) I found that both were very rigid and crunchy while rotating them. Her toes were also "hiding" under the fourth toe, meaning she was hiding aspects of her sexuality and creativity. Being an aspiring writer, she could use more release to unlock these toes. This in turn would make her creativity center more fluid and vital.

Interestingly enough, sometimes clients would manifest a new symptom right before coming to see me for the first time. This client reported having a breakout on her chin the morning before the first appointment. She said this had never happened, at least not in the last few years. The chin represents the facial corresponding area of the reproductive organs. Could it be that she started to actually respond to some energy stimulation prior to the actual session? Curiously, during the session I focused on the endocrine and reproductive reflexes. What is even more amazing is that at the time of the breakout on her chin she didn't even know she was going to see me as I had a client cancel at the last minute and I called to offer her the appointment. Her "reproductive breakout" might have even started before she actually consciously knew that she was going to be worked on. I must credit her with the fact that she brought this up and was able to make the connection herself. This could be an interesting example of synchronicity.

Ultimately, we are all connected by a thread of energy. I often witness clients who experience a sudden pain in the left knee before the first appointment. The left knee represents our left kidney and our past experience (if we are right handed) – as well as part of our fear/ego self. It even goes as far back as our past lives. So, it could be that before the healing session commences a part of us, an energetic part, picks up on the upcoming events before they even occur. A big ingredient of this healing work is to reconcile past and present, conscious and unconscious. The kidneys also represent the way in which we break down and process our emotional experiences. They also represent fear. Oftentimes a left knee pain can indicate knowingness or an awakening of some sort. I always say that I don't fix people. I simply allow an experience to come through. The client, in my eyes, does an equal amount of work by attending the session. It takes two.

So, it is beyond doubt that the more we open up our soles, the more flow is created and the more we become connected to ourselves, our souls. One of the main objectives of healing work has always been to help people "marry" their conscious and subconscious levels. By that I mean that many of us carry a gap or a conflict within us. It is as if our "awakened state" and "dream state" are not in contact with each other. Waking up in the morning with anger or fogginess can be an example of that. The bigger the gap between our awakened and dormant selves, the more frustrated and unfulfilled that we may feel. When our higher self is well merged and is in touch with our regular self, we feel more synchronicity. It is not about thinking too much – it is about flowing with inner guidance and intuition.

Our soles are the gateway for the knowledge of our souls. Not only do we release blocked energies in the healing work of reflexology, but blocked memories, as well. Blocked memories stem from this life and / or a past life and represent our emotional hang ups and fears. In a way, health means knowing where we came from and, therefore, where we are going to. It is no accident that the feet represent understanding. The Sole to Soul connection is a big secret of life.

~Part II: SOUL:
Our Density and Our Destiny~

Chapter Seven:
Energy Flow and Substance

Seeking the Peak Beyond

The totality of the events of our life may be seen as random; yet life may be too short for just that. The common denominator for all self realized people is the feeling that they are in synchronicity with life and the Universe. Abraham Maslow describes it as "peak episodes." People who seem to "have it all" (success, happiness, health) tend to report an occasional "communion with the divine." They simply get guidance from a higher Source. It could be that their higher Source is none other than their own openness to allow universal flow to go through them. This takes us back to the connection between body and mind, matter and energy, feet (below) and head (above). The more the "below" is opened up – the more harmony is dwelling in the "above." We are all conduits of energy. The less density we hold, the more we can flirt and flow with our own destiny.

Note the similarity between the words 'density' and 'destiny' – all the same letters, arranged differently. Amazing!

Much is said about self-love. One of the obstacles in psychotherapy is that the emotional body is hard to address in non organic manner. The emotional body is based on cellular memory that goes all the way back along our karmic path. Many of us carry some degree of fear as a key component in our karmic path. This fear is a major ingredient in our emotional body, regardless of how aware we are of it. In therapy, it can be hard to reach the emotional body by words alone, because our cellular memory often responds to physical stimulus as opposed to conversation only. It is as if words alone will not reach the memory of the body tissues. The feet serve as a great tool for this work since they represent our understanding. The English language affords us a glimpse into psycholinguistics. Under where we are standing lie the soles of our feet. So to understand means to have something flowing between us and Mother Earth! To understand means to be in alignment with a universal truth.

The more our daily life resembles the "program" of our higher self - the people we meet, the places we go to, the circumstances we encounter - the more likely we are to be self realized, or at least on an ongoing path of self-realization. We can become more and more frustrated when there are gaps between our higher self and our actual life. All this correspondence between the higher self and our daily reality comes down to our sugar and glucose management. This is because the more in synch we are in our life, the more in tune we are with the ultimate universal power of love. Therefore, the more in tune we are with love, the more balanced our sugar is. Sugar equals love! This marriage of the higher self and the actual life is manifested as self-realization. The more self realized we are, the more likely our blood sugar will be in balance. Once our feet are grounded and open to energetic flow from the Universe we are tuning in better to our higher selves.

In Kaballah God has a female counterpart called Shekhinah. While God is ever-present, his female counterpart only comes upon invitation. This union of the male / female aspect of the Divine is similar to the human state of self-realization. This union equates with having balance on all levels, "as above, so below." It is interesting to observe the location of the pancreas (our sugar regulator, connects to self-realization) in the body as it sits right by the waistline, our center point of balance. See Appendix I The Four Elements Chart of the Feet & The Emotions.

Chapter Eight:
Transformation and Change

Letting It Flow

Change can only happen when we let energy blockages flow out while manifesting the connection between our conscious and subconscious. In other words, all the elements should be cleared so that they can function as conduits of universal energy. It is our divine right to serve as a conduit of universal energy. All it takes is clearing the energy patterns that make it hard for the flow to happen. The Water element, the arch, is a major area where this unblocking takes place, for most blockages are rooted in our emotional self. As we see in The Toe Reading Chart—which can be found in Appendix II—our major emotions (such as fear, anger or joy) are located in the Water area of the feet. Opening up the elements allows us to eliminate all patterns of subconscious "less positive" emotions. As all patterns are opened, our natural restorative powers emerge.

67

A great way to understand energy dynamics is to look at yoga. The word *yoga* is derived from the Sanskrit word "yoge" meaning duality. The notion of two is a paramount in healing work. Two aspects or levels of being that exist at the same time and are approached simultaneously in order to make them more unified. The number two in healing usually refers to body and soul. Two can also represent our present / future versus our past, or our actual life versus our past life. Two is also our male/ female, resistance versus acceptance and "Good" versus "Bad." We observe that good and bad don't truly exist as we know them. What is "good" can actually prove to be very "bad" and vice versa. "Bad" things happen for a reason. They challenge our egos and make us grow; they move us out of our comfort zone. "Good" things on the other hand can keep us idle. We won't take measures to change ourselves if only good things happen to us. This is not to suggest that "good" is not good, but only to imply that there is more to it than a simple label.

Our immediate judgment
of "good" and "bad"
is often inaccurate.

There is also a "dangerous" implication when we judge someone or something as "negative." By making that judgment we imply that we or our things are the opposite or the "positive." By giving in to the dichotomy of negative vs. positive we actually give in to the duality of polarity instead of reinforcing the oneness of our Universe. So when we use the terms "good" and "bad" it's imperative that we remember to use caution.

A Course in Miracles teaches us that fear is the opposite of love, but since love is all there is fear's existence is an illusion in itself. In most cases, the ego-self can perceive reality only through dualities and opposites, without ever seeing through the oneness of it all. So, "negative" can be re-phrased as "something that is less positive." In other words all there is, is positivity, but in varying degrees. This "new" perception also allows us to step beyond black and white thinking and allow more shades of color to penetrate. This approach of "re-perceiving" reality simply helps us with seeing through the fragmentation and into a more unified and flowing way of living.

Sara's Story

"Sara" was a student at the college where I taught. She was suffering from an official case of arachnophobia (fear of spiders). Oddly, sometimes when she smiled I felt that her expression reminded me of a spider. One day while she was taking an exam she had to leave to the lady's room. While she was there washing her hands looking in the mirror, to her terror a big brown spider was sitting on her shirt, right over her solar plexus. She immediately brushed it off and ran with her last breath back to the exam room. This happened while Sara was seeing me for reflexology sessions. Sara's fear must have attracted the spider as it was sitting on her solar plexus, the seat of ego and fear. On another occasion, when she was in a hurry, she took a short cut through a bush in the parking lot just to bump into a giant spider web with a huge spider sitting right in the middle – making her face her fear head on! What we resist persists! When we open and let go of imbalances in our patterns - miracles and "coincidences" occur. This is how we heal along our spiritual path.

Chapter Nine:
Life Force and Past Issues

Revealing the Hidden

It would be interesting to examine what data we can draw from our ailments. The head is the mastermind. Many times we have problems in the head because the head represents the "above" of the "as above, so below" equation. This may indicate that the "below" is somewhat deficient because there is an imbalance. The "above" means our thoughts, aspirations and imagination. The "below" represents our grounding and our understanding. We have already seen that through contact with the ground our feet allow us to understand many things. Through the here and now we can comprehend. Think about the symbolism of the verb "to understand." It is under our stand, where we stand, how we stand! When things are under our stand we get them. ☺. This connection between standing and comprehension can also be found in other languages.

The more our past issues are unresolved, the less life force is available to us. One of the blockages in addressing a past issue is that they are hidden away from our consciousness. To this end they need to be brought up so we can deal with them. One of the foremost organs that help us bring about this change are the kidneys. The kidneys are the seat of our Jing - the energy that is given to us at birth through our DNA. Throughout life we need to disperse this energy wisely by aspiring to live a well balanced life; physically, emotionally, mentally and spiritually. The kidneys also represent the dispersion of our Chi - the immediate energy we derive from the breathing process. It is the kidneys that disperse the energy that flows from the lungs. In both cases of Chi and Jing, unresolved issues will cause us to compromise our life force. Every unresolved issue / trauma will end up in our "stress bank." It is like a deposit that creates debt instead of adding an asset.

Visualize a floating ship that keeps absorbing water into its compartments. It may not sink if only some of the compartments are flooded but should it come across a big storm those flooded compartments will become a big hindrance. Our goal is to empty those compartments so we can remain balanced and afloat. Usually we are not even aware of how flooded our compartments are. They, like our subconscious dwell mostly "under the water", hidden from our conscious emotions. One of the principles we need to remember is that density is the number one stumbling block in health. Density can be emotional, mental, physical or spiritual.

**The more density we carry
the less change can occur.
Hence, emptying ourselves of our density
is the key.**

The law of opposites "as above, so below" indicates that as we open the below (feet), we enable the above (head) to open up. In harmony, above and below become united. Head and feet connect with the Universe – the head connects to the infinite and the feet to the here and now. Some common manifestations of density are toxicity (for example, due to food toxins) and painful emotions (due to anger or fear). We can help by drinking more water and eliminating food additives such as preservatives, high fructose corn syrup and food dyes. It is a good idea to examine the option of eating according to our blood type. Some wonderful work has been done on how our blood type carries the needs of our make- up. Walking can also help to reduce density - and the same goes for laughter. Interestingly, laughter makes us less acidic.

Alex's Story

"Alex" came to me with gout in his right big toe which was red and swollen. He used to drink heavily which added to the problem as alcohol is primarily sugar and acidic substances. He was 44, a movie producer and a restaurant owner. He would get a gout attack every time he would get too stressed out. Our sessions were weekly. Alex would get interesting reactions just about every week. He would comment that his big toe improved, but then an area on his legs would swell up for no apparent reason. First it was his right knee, then the right ankle, then left ankle. It was fascinating to observe that every new swelling took away the swelling from his right toe. This went on for ten weeks.

After Alex stopped coming to see me, he left me a short message saying that his swelling disappeared. Why exactly his body decided to manifest random swelling in random areas is a mystery. The fact is that with each new swelling the real problem subsided, as if there were some compensatory mechanism in his body. Sometimes during the healing process things get worse before they get better, it's called a healing crisis. Often problems in one side of the body will manifest in the opposite side for a short time. This clearly is proof that the body knows just what to do. It

73

could do it by itself, but often an intervention is needed to "spin the wheel", which means to get something moving. In an ideal world we should be able to spin our own wheels without intervention, yet when stress patterns set in we sometimes need an intervention.

Conscious, Subconscious and Super Conscious

As we go along in life, the conscious level is our most accessible level of awareness. The conscious is also very much in line with our ego self. Therefore, ego / mind taint our conscious level with many perceptions. Our perceptions go back to how we have seen the world starting at a very early age. It is said that by age four, 40% of our life perceptions are already established. This means that many of our thoughts, choices and actions are based on events that happened before we turned four years old. Some say that a child by that age still has recollection or memories of past life events. Regardless if we accept this or not, I am certain that we have been affected by what we saw, heard, and felt at a young age.

So, the reason why you are reading this book may be because you're open to different points of view so that you can derive inspiration and enrich your life experience. How are you living your life? Are you "living dangerously"? Are you taking risks? How ready are you to step out of your comfort zone? Having a healthy intuition helps us to step out of our comfort zone. Living courageously and taking risks will lead us to cultivate a richer living and therefore lead to the ideal life that we dreamed for ourselves. A recent study conducted about longevity compared 50 variables regarding exercise, geographical location, nutrition, sexual activity, etc. The results were astonishing! It was discovered that the most dominant indicator of longevity was the degree to which there was "intricacy and completion" in one's life. Amazingly, those who lived easier lives seemed to have a shorter lifespan than those who successfully dealt with challenge and hardship. A big factor in dealing with life's challenges – or "living dangerously" - is to cultivate intuition. This means to allow the deepest levels of awareness, the subconscious, to permeate the surface of consciousness.

There are three levels of awareness: conscious, subconscious and super-conscious. The subconscious is a bridge between the conscious and super-conscious. Our happiness, our choices and our actions will all benefit from having more access to our super-conscious. Cultivating more access to our intuition is the key. Our dreaming can be a great getaway to the deeper levels of our being. Being grounded in the here and now is the key to being well connected with our super-conscious. This is in total compliance with the principle of "as above, so below." We can only attain balance when we are rooted in the present with love and grace, and at the same time be in touch with our deeper self through our intuition. Note that the subconscious is intimately connected to the super-conscious. Therefore, accessing the subconscious will automatically affect the access to our super-conscious.

Chapter Ten:
Ego and the Comfort Zone

The Enemies of Intuition

Our mind, our ego and our perceptions will try to sabotage our inner voice. They will all try to "write off" our creative higher faculties because they just don't "make sense." The conscious mind (our ego reality) is not readily capable of connecting directly with our super-conscious mind (our higher divine self). Yet, using the subconscious as a bridge, the super-conscious can feed the conscious mind with inspiration and intuition hence the subconscious is a bridge to our higher self.

It is through this connection of above and below
– Super-conscious and conscious –
that an integrated life is truly available to us.

Making this connection is easier said than done. Life

presents all kinds of situations that can aggravate us and force our ego to come out. When we are aggravated we can be thrown off balance and often become reactive. The more reactive we get, the more chance we get to encounter our ego with its insane narrowness and lack of creativity. Creativity encourages change and a fear of change is caused by our attachment to ego.

There is a direct link between our comfort zone and our attachment to our illusionary self; the ego. The ego's intention is mainly to keep the existing situation as it is. The more changes we allow, the more growth will be possible. To change is to shift and in order to shift we must step out of our comfort zone. We are not likely to voluntarily step out of our comfort zone because that would break the illusion our ego works so hard to maintain to ensure its survival.

Being in the present is the key to identifying ego response and allowing introspection. Our comfort zone can become a fool's paradise, an illusionary state of being where we are constantly defending a faulty perception of the self. We can use the same energy to observe the many instances that life presents to us to grow, to be creative, to share ourselves and to invite more and more of our higher selves into this very moment.

On Vitality and Releasing Blockages

Many times a certain blockage in the body "holds up" our vitality. Old feelings and sensations can have curative properties. For example, if we used to bathe in the ocean or swimming pool as children and haven't done so in a long time, doing so may invoke the same purifying feeling we experienced before. Having our feelings "regressed" has even far more healing properties. Immediately following a healing session, we often find that a client's facial expression changes tremendously. I often notice that my client's facial age seems to have reduced substantially, that they appear younger. I normally take a guess as to what age these specific facial expressions represent and what it means that we have tapped into the energy and state of mind different than what the client feels at the moment. Usually the current facial expression we carry contains within it pain, disappointment and stress. Once the body is in this state it can reverse different expressions, usually to the ones we had prior to existing trauma.

For example "Rachel", a 46 year old woman who had just gone through a divorce, her house was sold and her friends dispersed between her and her ex husband. When she came to me she had a smile on her face but otherwise seemed so stressed out. It held so much pain and no focus. It seemed to me as if she was saying, "I'm smiling because I don't want to cry." After only three sessions, Rachel looked into the mirror in my office and made the comment that, "This is the 'me' like I used to be." I couldn't negate the dramatic difference apparent in her expression.

This doesn't necessarily mean that the person will carry these new expressions from now on and let go of all their stress forever. Rather, these expressions reflect that the hundreds of facial muscles connected with our inner essence and cellular memory are a projection of the changes we experience. I would say that I have witnessed these "expression miracles" in many of the clients I see. One can contend that this change in expression is a part of the reconnection with the subconscious mind. One thing is to feel relaxed after a session, but it is another thing entirely to feel different, to look into the mirror and say, "Wow, now this is me!" or "This is how I was ten years ago."

A great ingredient in allowing all this to happen is to take time to reflect and just be. It is interesting to note that every time we reconnect with the inner-self we tend to manifest some release from the Water element (the emotions). This release often comes in the form of some loose bowel movements that are accompanied by a noticeable odor. This is usually a sign of physiological and emotional release. Remember that this area of the body, namely the lower abdomen, is our blind spot area. The Water element covers the space between the abdomen and the abdominal floor, between bottom of ball of foot and beginning of heel. It is divided in half by the waistline. Anything above the waistline is more conscious where below is less conscious. Interestingly enough, in Hebrew this area is called the blind intestine. This area is where we turn a blind eye to ourselves. Not necessarily by a conscious choice. It is by releasing trapped energy in the subconscious area (large intestine) that one is able to be more conscious of present events and reflect on them.

It is not an accident that the food we eat represents, metaphysically, the ideas that we have to process and digest. By transmuting our subconscious ideas into our consciousness we are capable of living a happier life, full of synchronicity and wonder. Things start to fall into place better; there is a better sense of timing. Dreams can become more vivid, symbolic and mysterious. "Coincidence" occurs more often.

Releasing our blockages and digesting our hidden thoughts doesn't mean that from now on everything in our life will be easy, but it means that we'll have greater chance to be aware of the dimensions that surround us - including being better able to hear our inner voice and our higher self.

Life as a Forest of Symbols

The symbolic life holds an ability to recognize patterns and signs that unify us in a universal existence. Every thought, dream and aspiration can be seen through the symbol prism. Under "symbols" we include archetypes, elements, patterns and any other representation of various aspects of our life. Our lives can seem chaotic, yet if we take a closer look we can identify symbols that can be utilized for our greater benefit. It is not that each second we need to search for a sign or a symbol, but when we happen upon an unusual occurrence or object there's probably an inherent message in that very moment. These messages can be seen as the Universe's affirmation of our desires or concerns.

The word Universe means "one version/vibration" because "all is one" in the Universe.

Our false sense of separation from each other and our world only exists because of our ego identification with our physical reality. This sense of separation is only as real as we allow it to be. Life as a whole can be reasoned as a journey to regain that sense of oneness. We travel this journey in spite of and through our ego identification. The friction between our ego-centered sense of reality and the true reality of oneness forces us to rediscover the interconnectedness inherent within the Universe. In the same way that our prayers are answered, the more we notice the interconnectedness - the more synchronized our lives become. In a synchronized life, good and bad no longer exist as absolutes. We realize there are many shades of color between black and white.

The ego thrives on separation from the unity of interconnectedness. Nothing inflicts more suffering than the ego mind. The ego is contractive and the higher self is expansive. Only the higher self connects us to the universal truth that all is one. It is important to note that the access to the ego and higher self are not absolutes, are not black and white. Every day is a journey in overcoming ego and reconnecting to the higher self. Oftentimes as we advance our consciousness' unknown reserves of ego, it will attempt to spurt out and threaten our progress. It is important to be in the moment and not give power to the untiring efforts of the ego. Life is symbolic. We are our symbols. Symbolism is a poetic way to observe our journey. What role are we playing? Contemplating our own symbols, archetypes and core lessons – from self-mastery to being healing agents for ourselves and others - is the key to realizing that our life is a journey in a Forest of Symbols.

Jenny's Story

"Jenny" is 43 years old and employed as a nanny. Her past occupations have been mostly those of physical labor, but she doesn't exercise at all. She has suffered from ankle injuries on various occasions although she walks a great deal in her job. She has also suffered from blood pressure issues for some period of time. Her childhood was a difficult one since she assumed the role of second mother to her siblings while her mother went to work. She also had an absent father.

Jenny has a great deal of problems sleeping completely through the night, doesn't record dreams and her nerves are rather frazzled due to financial pressures. She cannot have any cloth over her face while she sleeps since she has anxiety attacks. She avoids small enclosed areas and can't relax for long periods of time. Jenny doesn't have any alcohol or smoking habits, but is compulsive in her diet. She also has chronic headaches and is very nervous in nature. Jenny feels a great need to help others while she grants herself second consideration. She keeps very good hygiene although her style of dress is disorganized and not very thought out.

She had two children through natural childbirth. About fifteen years ago her son died in an automobile accident. Shortly thereafter, her husband passed away from a heart attack as a result of resuming his drinking habit. The first few years after her losses, she suffered from severe depression and a desire to die. As the years have passed her condition has somewhat improved. She still has one child who is currently twenty years old. She is presently living with someone she met a few years after her husband's death. He also suffered a loss of a close person in his life. This gave them a common ground of understanding.

During our sessions we focused on her unresolved grief issues and therefore emphasized the lung area. When we work on the lung area we not only release grief, but we also open paths to soul connection and past lives. Related to this connection, after a few sessions Jenny had a vision of a jaguar walking around my office. Towards the end of the session she saw the jaguar approaching her and staring into her eyes. She didn't feel any fear when the jaguar approached her, yet she was impressed greatly by the vision. She continued to see images of the jaguar days after the session. A few sessions later she saw an image of a Native American woman walk by and glance at her. At another time she saw an image of an eagle staring at her as well. These visions could be universal symbols or actual recollections of her past lives.

Throughout the sessions Jenny's attitude and outlook improved as well as her ability to have a healthy night's sleep. Her friends and family noticed she had a new manner about herself in how she related to her life. She was more grounded and less prone to sacrifice herself for others. The metaphor in Jenny's vision is staggering. The jaguar and Native American woman symbolize universal power and Jenny's ability to heal herself. In Native American shamanism the jaguar is a dominant creature of the tropical forest and the guardian of the gates of the afterlife. It also helps erase the parts of us that no longer serve us and helps us advance in our lives. The eagle represents clarity, vision and foresight. It brings transcendental beginnings. We are elevated above our dilemmas on the wings of the eagle and it allows us to see our lives with perspective. Knowing Jenny's traumas, symbols are extremely significant and proved helpful in her healing.

Shapes of the Ego

Our physical world, the world of forms, only represents a part of our reality. Because nothing can truly exist without energy to sustain it, our physical world is a partial reality. If we identify completely with it we lose the access to its energetic essence. There always exists a dialogue between the physical and non-physical. This is the same dialogue as between "above and below." Everything corresponds to everything else in a unified world, yet the ego resents unification by striving for complete separation. One mechanism to overcome ego identification is transcendence. Once we acknowledge our identification with ego we have the potential to engage in the process of shifting. Transcendence means the ongoing process of shifting our awareness. One underlying emotion that is always present with ego is fear. We can have fear of death, fear of loss, fear of gain, fear of just about everything. In an unexamined existence, our lives swing between the fear of being alive in the here-and-now and the fear of death. Fear seems to be everywhere.

The ego is so manipulative
that it will relentlessly seek new venues
of intimidation through fear
so that it can justify its existence.

The 7 Chakras system is a model where different body parts resonate with different aspects of the human experience and its connection to the universe. In this system, the ego projects on the third Chakra (Solar Plexus – front center bottom of ribcage) and thus the conditional aspects of love which need to transform and manifest as unconditional love in the fourth Chakra (the heart). This is foreign to the Universe which only acts in unconditional love. This boundary between conditional and unconditional love is the essence of the journey we are here to take. Moreover, the lower Chakras - one, two and three - are connected to our basic "fight or flight" existence, a state we share with other creatures. From the fourth Chakra and above we enter the realm of the higher existence; it is state of being capable of making miracles happen and making suffering cease. See the Chakra Chart in Appendix X.

Also, the higher we go in the Chakra system, the more we move away from ego identification into our universal and divine selves. One prevailing misperception is that it is "wrong" to be in our ego self, yet, just as all our Chakras need to be open so do we have to acknowledge all of our aspects before we can even attempt to shift and transcend. Often transcendence is nearly impossible unless the body itself is open. The body's open resistance can be the ultimate weapon against the ego's efforts. Mind-body is not just a cliché statement; both aspects of self have to be worked on in order to live a fulfilled life.

Transcendence and Well Being

People who have undergone mystical experiences are psychologically better off in terms of well being. In a way, mystical experiences are essential to facilitate the shift from an ego based life to a more spiritualized life. This is because mystical experiences connect us to the Source, the Universe. Beyond the importance of cultivating intuition, we are all able to draw a mystical component into our lives, without compromising our sense of normalcy. Note that the ego is very linear whereas the higher self is not. There shouldn't be a battle between the two. It is possible to use your linear faculties to attain some aspects of self realization. It will take non-linear aspects in order to have it all.

Be open to the different, sometimes unexpected, channels through which the Universe will attempt to reach you. No channel is too high or too low for this purpose. Affirmations are a great channel to create a dialogue with the Universe. The ego objects affirmations because they threaten to shift its very existence. When we affirm often a conflict emerges- an inner voice of doubt. It is important to work with this voice and subdue it. Once we allow a mystical component to take place in our lives without labeling or compartmentalizing it we allow for the universal channels to open and flow freely. From the soul's standpoint, the ego is the night time of the soul - where fear and darkness reign. However, it is by understanding our fears that we can actually bring more day-light to our lives. We also shift our ego by acting on and responding to others' needs – not just our own. To know what the needs of others are we need to use common sense and more importantly intuition.

Cultivating Intuition

How many times have you, in retrospect, felt you should have acted on your gut-feelings and intuitions? We are usually aware of our intuitive impulses, but often our linear mind doubts their validity. One component for cultivating intuition is imagining that within us, no matter what, we always have an open space available for any possibility to enter. If we live like we are completely full, hardly anything non-linear can come our way. Imagine your life as a dresser. In a full dresser, you may know exactly what is in each drawer, but even if you don't - it is still cluttered. It is harder to manifest a better life when our drawers are all full.

As an exercise, close your eyes and visualize a dresser with full drawers. In your mind imagine trying to fit anything into those full drawers, it's impossible. Now try to empty one of your drawers or just keep very few things there and make an agreement with yourself to always keep this one drawer empty. Focus on that one empty drawer and – even with all the drawers closed - know there is nothing there. Know that this empty drawer will allow for the new and, sometimes, undefined to enter your life. Sit with it, allow the sensation of it. Now, open your eyes and begin to notice how holding this empty space projects itself into your actual life. This is an exercise in reducing density in our lives which is the pre-requisite for increasing our intuition.

Acting on our gut feelings is another great way to be in sync with our intuition. I was recently at a seminar on a cruise ship. The ship was scheduled to leave the current port in forty minutes. I was already seated in a classroom reflecting on a gift item I had just purchased on shore for a friend. I liked it so much I was thinking that I should go back and buy one for myself, but, I figured I shouldn't go as it would take at least twenty five minutes to go purchase it and return. Yet my inner voice kept insisting that I go. I rushed out of the seminar leaving behind my notebook on the small table and made it back just in time before the boat departed. Yet, to my surprise, when I returned to the classroom - two women were now sitting at my table. I excused myself, gathered my stuff and squeezed in by the end of the table. As I sat there, I was wondering where on earth they came from and how they had pushed aside my belongings on the table and why they decided to sit there in the first place. My initial reaction was anger because they left very little space for me to sit next to them. I felt slightly violated by their behavior.

Eventually I got over my hurt and smiled at the lady next to me. As the conversation ensued, I realized how essential it was for us to talk as she had some very special messages for me. It was a magical moment which became more magical as our connection continued. She was telling me about a man she had met earlier that day. She said she was going to have dinner with him later. Sometime after dinner that night, her dining companion gave me a call on her referral. This man subsequently proved very instrumental to a project I was working on. A project that I had spoken of with the women seated next to me earlier that day. The woman who, at first, seemed to be a bother to me but in reality meeting her was a blessing.

I kept wondering about the urge to leave the ship earlier and how it was unlikely I would have spoken to that woman if I hadn't. I listened carefully to everything she told me—and obviously she listened carefully to me—and I realized that our meeting was not accidental. If we want to cultivate intuition, we must pay attention to these types of unique and sometimes bothersome situations. As a matter of fact, the times we feel aggravated are the times when we should pay attention the most. Think of it as a pathway to moving out of your comfort zone to where you can use your intuition to see your situation differently.

Listen to the messages of your inner voice
– your intuition –
and follow its wisdom.

Forgiveness

Part of emptying the drawer to leave space for our intuition to emerge can be achieved through forgiveness. A big chunk of our inner chatter has to do with unresolved life situations. Forgiveness can help to let go of the "he said, she said" chit-chat and allow us to clear the drawer to make space for the new. Ultimately many memories and resentments go back to the ego whose supreme antidote is forgiveness. Interestingly enough, the colon or large intestine represents forgiveness in holism. When the colon is physiologically detoxified—as through colonics or cleanses—it parallels emptying the drawer and releasing clutter that no longer serves us.

If forgiveness proves hard to come by, visualize a forgiven world where sincere apologies and kind actions replace all misgivings. Notice that our attachment to past events is a stumbling block to our growth. I am not recommending that we quickly rush to forgive. Doing so can turn out to be simply lip service and is not a sincere release of blame. Instead, aim attention at engaging in the process of forgiveness where our heart and mind both take part. This may take longer, but it will be more authentic. Set your intention with love. The intention to forgive will by itself open the pathway to forgiveness and aid in the release of blame.

Debby's Story

"Debby" is a 52 year old accountant who is a survivor of incest. When we first met, her facial features were somewhat masculine. Her toes had a very irregular pattern in that each toe pointed in a different direction. Sometimes a deep childhood trauma deeply affects the Air element which is located in the toes and seen to represent our mental growth. I emphasize her toes as I assume that they bear the memories of the traumas she suffered in her youth.

Within a few sessions Debby started to have symbolic dreams. In one of them she was riding in a car with her friend who drove accidentally into a private property. When they noticed the mistake they attempted to leave the property, but the only way out was through a private garage. As they entered the garage, an older man at the window pressed a button and repeatedly slammed the garage door on the car so they couldn't leave. Debby woke up in a sweat as a result of this episode. She told me that this man reminded her of her father in some ways.

A few weeks later Debby reported having a dream. In her dream, she was sleeping in a queen size bed. Also in the dream, she awoke to find herself glancing over to the other side of the bed only to discover melting lava where a potential partner might have been. I asked her what the lava meant to her and she said it was probably a Fire symbol that corresponded to anger that she felt about all the relationships in her life and, specifically, a lack of a loving partner.

For the first time she felt the connection between her challenges with committed relationships and what took place with her father so many years prior. Debby was beginning the process of forgiving. She had set her loving intention by starting healing sessions. She was gaining a sense of awareness and connection in her life that was having an effect on the way she showed up in the world. She said that two of her girlfriends told her she looked more feminine as a result of the sessions.

Cultivating Forgiveness

What often holds us back from releasing our ego is our lack of forgiveness. While there is meaning to owning each moment of our experience, it is part of our soul work to constantly release those experiences. Only people who carry pain in themselves will want to hurt us. Loving them - and thanking them for the experience - will release our attachment to the event. Our self-esteem is greatly affected by other people's judgment toward us. Once we establish an inner core, a peaceful center that is ours only and no one else can enter, we realize that at that moment we heal our misperceptions and judgments of others. These misperceptions and judgments are fear projections onto others. They can only affect us as much as we carry the same fears in us. Some common examples are: fear of inadequacy, fear of ridicule, fear of not being good enough.

Stop and think; the past is a fact - we can't change the facts. Yet, just because it happened, it does not mean it needs to linger. Only we can reflect on it and derive the best answers to make our life better now. Only we can learn to nurture ourselves and attract what we need. By releasing our attachment to the past we allow the infinite wisdom of the Universe to permeate and heal us. Our attachment to the past affects the way we breathe and even the flow of our bowel movements! It is known that constipation is often a symptom of not being able to let go.

As adults, we can't blame our parents for what we have or have not become. To do so, means that we take no responsibility for our thoughts, feelings and actions. Besides, we can't change the past. Our past is our point of departure - definitely not our destination. The more challenging our past was the more fuel in our engine. More power to you! Embrace the beautiful nature of the "good and bad" polarity. Nothing can be very bad unless it is so perceived by us. Our perception judges it all as good or bad. The fact is that some of our worst experiences can be the best things to ever happen to us - a wake-up call like no other!

Three Steps to Cultivate Forgiveness

1. Think of an experience in your life where you felt emotional pain. Observe the feeling.
2. Give thanks to the circumstance of the experience - for bringing you the experience and the pain and discomfort it caused in your life.
3. Give thanks to the people involved in the experience – including you. Thank everyone involved for their participation in bringing you a necessary life lesson.

Congratulations, you have just gotten closer to release a pattern that does not serve you well. Giving thanks releases you from the need to repeat these experiences in this life and other life times. It will help to connect your ego self to your higher self. It is important to note that from the ego's standpoint there is nothing to thank for. How can we thank people/events that hurt us? Remember, this is an exercise in soul evolution. The soul does not judge "good" or "bad." This judgment is the good old ego's job.

Cultivating Courage - Exploring from Within

Many answers are given once we are on the path of self-realization. The main ingredient with which most self knowledge manifests is courage. We can have all the answers, yet paralysis can still stifle our acting. Thought without action is incomplete. Courage is the ability to act without knowing what the results will be ahead of time. Courage is the bridge from frustration to self-realization. It is the stepping out of time and from that moment of eternity, acting / speaking in a way that embodies love, compassion and wisdom. Courageous actions inspire and encourage our experience of belonging, worth and fearlessness. Wisdom is a collection of courageous actions that bring forth the way of being that is the source of all phenomena.

Actions that lessen suffering express our unity.

Five Steps to Becoming Courageous

These five practices when carried out with trust create a more courageous and authentic life.
1. Join in and embody a life story bigger than your own comfort and survival.
2. Learn by examining your experiences and stories about your fears.
3. Build competence - by using your will - to stay present and act when afraid.
4. Practice faith and patience - take positive action even when you see no positive outcome immediately, soon or ever.
5. Pat yourself on the shoulder and acknowledge when you feel that you acted courageously and more and more acts of courage will manifest in your life.

By living a story bigger than our own comfort and survival we tell the Universe that we are able to expand our reality and that we don't identify with the limitations imposed on us by the fear-based ego. If fear was the opposite of courage then by examining how fear plays a role in our life events we re-examine our choices and see to what extent fear truly affects our decisions. The most common reaction to fear is not being in the moment. Examine how you are staying present in times of fear. Notice your breathing patterns and your overall balance in order to attain a firmer grip on that moment. Then you will begin to release your attachment to patterns of fear.

All this is possible through cultivation of faith and patience. Act upon your heart's impulses in spite of what your logic tells you. These positive action patterns establish a dialogue with the Universe where doors are opened as we move beyond our ego's limitations. In developing courage our existence becomes a part of a greater picture; one that extends beyond our own life in direct relation to others and the world. As our vision expands we connect with the oneness, the unity and the interconnectedness that is the source of all phenomena.

Love is an action, not just a feeling.

Chapter Eleven:
Emotional Flow

Locating the Pain

Recall a painful experience you had, one that you have not forgotten. Now locate the spot in your body that corresponds to this feeling. Very often, the seat of our body pain is in the abdomen - right over the intestines, but any location of pain in the body may have a meaning. In this example, the abdomen is the location of the subconscious, of letting go and of forgiveness. Every location in our body carries a meaning. We need to let go of our attachment to our painful experiences in order to become more authentic. They define us in as much as our name does, but we are better served if we can accept that there is an identity for us free of attachment to pain. The phrase "let go and let god" sums it up. Agree to let go of your pain even when you feel you don't know how to. Intention counts! Release any contract you have made to endorse suffering as it hinders well being. Ease of being is possible, as "ease" not "dis-ease" is our natural state.

Owning all our experiences also pertains to the bringing in of people to our lives including family members, as choices we have made on a karmic level. Now, send love and thanks to them for presenting you with valuable lessons on your journey of self discovery. When we thank everything and everyone, we untie our pain from our body and allow new experiences of love and gratitude to flow. Human nature is such that if we have nine "good" experiences and one "bad" experience, we will tend to dwell on the single bad one. Sit comfortably and reflect on a gracious moment or event that happened to you. See how self worth, self respect and well being fill you up. What you dwell on becomes reality. Allow the gracious moments in your life to be your beacon. Your becoming a whole being depends on your emotional body's shift from pain-consciousness to light-consciousness. The more love and light we connect with, the more we'll dissolve the pain body and allow for our higher self to flow in. See The Four Elements Chart of the Feet & The Emotions in Appendix I for a foot map of emotions and their respective organs.

Removing Grief, Fear, Guilt and Anger and Inviting Joy and Passion In

Grief

Grief feeds on a sense of loss. A sense of loss feels like we will never be able to retrieve something we lost. It can be a lost childhood, parent, youth, etc. In this mindset a loss is absolute, just like death. A good approach to overcoming grief is to examine our attachments and the meaning of what and who is "ours." As we tap into the universal truth that nothing is ours and everything is transient, we can gradually reconfigure the faulty perception of loss. This issue draws directly on the energy matter paradigm: the more we move from ego perception to a higher self understanding, the more we connect with energies that exist beyond physical reality.

When we do this we decrease our sense of loss. In this very moment, we can turn "loss" into a perception as opposed to a fact. Loss is a false attachment to the world of forms. This process takes time and can be painful. However, remind yourself on a constant basis that there is a reality beyond that which the eye can see. This is not to underestimate valid experiences that left us in grief. Grief stifles the soul. We are referring to the understanding that grief is an emotion that is harmful when not released. We can't change the events, yet we can change our perception of them. This change will result in having less suffering and more joy. Less grief = More joy.

Fear

In fear there are unprocessed emotions, for fear itself is contraction – a state in which nothing can be processed well. Fear makes us dense, contracted and undiscerning. We need to trust that we can process all of our experiences and learn from them. If we are truly a mirror of higher universal dynamics then we can only respond to that which is expansive. Fear is resisting this expansive motion as if it's trying to establish a dimension for itself, a dimension that only exists within the ego. Fear is the manifestation of the ego's insistence to narrow the scope in which we see reality. Fear resists the natural flow in our life and is attached to time and space. *A Course in Miracles* teaches that time and space are both born when we symbolically and collectively fall from energy into matter. This fall is a metaphor for a choice to deny energy and define reality by matter alone. The key is to acknowledge that time and space are perceptions. The way out of fear consciousness is to challenge our linear thinking and allow a higher miraculous Source to intervene. This will re-balance our ego perceptions with the infinite vibrations of the cosmos. As fear makes us dense and undiscerning, we need to trust that we can process all of our experiences and learn from them.

Guilt

Guilt is an overlap of unresolved emotions, namely fear grief and shame. It stands as a blockage between our ego-self and our higher-self. Guilt is very close to grief – a feeling of loss and wrong-doing exacerbated by the inability to process it. Guilt also feeds on shame - both build up like a cancer in our soul. It implies that no forgiveness is great enough to dissolve it. The key to handling guilt is forgiveness and compassion for others and self.

Anger

Anger is rooted in fear and guilt, but essentially anger is a cry for help, a cry for assistance. We get angry when we allow ourselves to be subjected to the unbalancing forces of the ego. When we are angry at ourselves or another we have forgotten how to forgive. But, when we allow our life to be balanced through embracing our spiritual connectivity to the Universe we cultivate forgiveness and reduce anger. Forgiveness requires stepping out of the linear perception of time, place and circumstance. Forgiveness is the key to opening blockages in our mind, body and spirit. Nothing is black and white and everything is a process, but with conscious intention one can let go and release anger – even about the most difficult issues to forgive.

**Forgiveness is
letting go of the forces of the ego
and instead being in the here-and-now.**

98

Joy

To cultivate joy, release grief. Seek out nature. It is not an accident that there is so much green in nature. Green is the color of the heart Chakra and plants are conduits of heart energy. In nature there exists a correspondence between energy, the hidden, and matter, the apparent. The birds that sing are very present in-the moment just as many phenomena in nature are in the here-and-now. Seek out the song of nature in any form and joy will manifest more in your life. Mother earth is joyful. Try a simple technique for grounding, which is purposefully connecting your feet to the earth, dirt, grass, sand, etc. Simply walk bare foot! Grounding reduces density, centers us, and connects us to our joy. Rejoice!

Passion

Passion connects to joy and expression. To cultivate passion, try to remember what you liked to do when you were eight or nine years old! Often those activities hold the key to remembering our passion. Try to remember who you were before puberty. What was your passion? Very often passion and creativity go hand in hand. As a child you had infinite potential for creation. Tapping into our creative potential is a key in arousing our passion. Passion is stifled by criticism. Nothing is as important as our self critique. Look at the ways you criticize yourself and distinguish between constructive criticism and self talk that is stifling your spirit. Passion is love in action. It's the merging of heart and mind.

The Releasing Breath

The gateway to healing goes through releasing grief and

acting on forgiveness. The emotion of grief correlates to the lungs in TCM (Traditional Chinese Medicine). The lungs also connect to the large intestine (letting go, forgiveness).The lungs correspond to our connection with Spirit. In every breath that we take we are respiring (re-spire: reconnecting with the Spirit), and it is essential to clear the pathway and do the healing, so to create an even flow between body and spirit. Breathing doesn't just mean the way we inhale / exhale; rather it entails how much space truly exists in our lungs physiologically and emotionally. In other words, with unresolved grief we are likely to have impaired breathing of some sort due to old muscle contractions. In a technical lab analysis of our lungs, these patterns may not show up. Many people breathe below their optimal capacity and may not even be aware of it.

There exists an ebb and flow, a process of breathing, between all the five energy centers represented in the toes. Examining the toes can serve for the purpose of understanding the emotional flow. It is also important to understand the relationship and dynamics among grief, fear, anger, joy and passion. Our energy flows through the traits and attributes of each center. Note the location of the lungs and colon in the top of the hierarchy on The Toe Reading Chart in Appendix II.

Smoking is a major vice that is very difficult to quit. Very often when we choose the smoking veil to come between us and our grief it's as if in the very moment when the lungs are filled with smoke we can tap into the essence of our grief. We can only reach it through a smoke screen. Smoking also involves the lips and the primordial sucking instinct which activates the peristalsis in the digestive tract to include the large intestine, an organ that pairs with the lungs. Therefore, smoking could be an ideal digestive aid if it weren't for its toxic side effects and damage.

To truly release grief patterns and invoke more space to contain the soul, we want to clear out toxins. It is not an accident that heavy metals count as some of the more toxic substances we absorb. The Metal element is connected to grief and can also affect

100

our behavior. I sometimes hear clients say they had a metallic smelling bowel movement following a session. Sometimes it's a metallic taste in the mouth. In either case, our body chemistry, the nutrients we absorb and the toxins we release play an important role in our health. There is a theory that each part in the intestinal tract corresponds to a different part in the body. Dried fecal matter can accumulate and clog the system. Years of chronic constipation can lead to a clogged system. Body cleansing systems are a good option as we really want to improve our ability to absorb what really feeds us and release what doesn't. As food corresponds to all the ideas we need to "digest," opening up areas of constipation, stagnation and toxicity can increase the flow of life. We need to acknowledge our attachment to pain and grief or it will persist.

What we resist persists.

Our ability to breathe well is a good gauge to how well we exchange energies with the world. Grief is an ultimate stumbling block in the flow of breathing. Grief limits the ability of the lungs to breathe and absorb fresh nutrients. Just like breathing represents how present our soul is - it also corresponds to the flow of infinite energy in our life because air is an infinite substance. Theoretically speaking, if we send a beam of light into space it will go on forever. The point is that air is infinite. As an element, Air has no limitation and no boundaries.

Forgiveness allows for joy to flow into the heart. The attachment to habit is connected to the heart center in that the heartbeat represents repetition. When we allow habit to joyfully shift according to our current needs we allow emotional flow and more balance. The kidneys represent emotional filtration in that they filtrate and purify our emotional experiences and keep only that which serves us. It is important to filter our experiences - keeping the valuable lessons while tossing what doesn't benefit us any longer. In a joyful mindset there is more emotional balance and well being. Anger has no place in such a state. Creativity and wonder move in to make for a complete cycle of soul-based living. Grief attaches itself to soul and its removal is a key condition for the soul to manifest in our lives.

Understanding the Emotions

The instinctive urge to survive guides our life from its inception. Fear defines our emotional range through its manifested emotions such as shame, anger, terror, frustration and guilt. All human emotions can be explained through the prism of fear, for fear has different sub-emotions and links to a wide array of experiences. The emotion of terror is deep, unresolved fear. It connects to our basic existential needs. When we experience basic needs that are not fulfilled or violently denied in childhood, we often turn into fearful and unconfident adults. We tend to have unexplained fears stemming from the past although we will not necessarily remember our childhood and may describe it as a "blackout."

Unfulfilled basic needs in childhood, such as love and security, influence the rest of our lives. When we don't know how to deal with or channel this issue, we can face situations in which we perceive certain intense feelings on an existential level, as in death related feelings. Ideally, we would pause and reflect in "real time" on this perceived threat. But since emotions are anchored in the Water element, intense fear tends to act like a wave coming from these deep seated unfulfilled needs. When this happens terror becomes violence. We act as if we are fighting to survive when in reality it is a perceived threat. Just like fear is ego related and based in perception, violence connects to terror and perceives a threat to our existence. This ability to be violent explains how otherwise "nice people" can commit "a crime of passion" and act as if this jealousy invoked their innermost existential fears. They often act out of feelings as if they are fighting for their life. Not having our basic needs met in childhood can be very powerful in shaping our perception and mode of operation [M.O.] as adults. It greatly contributes to our fear - pain body.

It's important to recognize that it's rare to have all our basic needs met in childhood. It is never too late to compensate for these lacks later in life. For example, a deficient father figure (father left or died or was not available) can affect the way we perceive God and have faith in life. This reminds one of "God Our Father." I have observed many times that when a man has a weak father figure he could have a crisis with faith and sometimes have unhandled anger. Others of us have mothers who are not nurturing and this can manifest itself as misunderstanding of the feminine principle, such as nurturing and intuition.

It is essential to know that any unfulfilled basic needs could manifest in our adult life as fear on different levels - from mild to wild! When we refuse to experience fear, we can experience anxiety. Anxiety is not as existential as terror, but it has to do with a refusal to look within. Anxiety is physically expressed by palpitations, dry mouth, dilated pupils and muscle contractions, to name some. When under anxiety, we shorten our breathing.

**Breathing has to do with
how much we really want
to be here and now.**

Self-realization is the ultimate answer to residues we carry. When we are self realized, we are in the now; acting on what is right - good for us. Otherwise, the option is frustration. Frustration is a conflict between our actual manifested life and our higher self picture we hold of ourselves. Frustration is also the gap between our ego's perception of life and our higher self. It is always our higher self that "nags" and wants us to remember who we truly are. Life is such that we move into a comfort zone, just to leave it and "jump into the water" again in search for the next comfort zone. The reason for not staying too long in a comfort zone is that growth is only possible by emerging from it. Comfort zones are not static; they are simply stepping stones, a part of the journey. Fear is always present and our courage would determine how we accept a temporary lack of comfort. Being aware of fear is powerful; when befriending our fear, we get to know what motivates it and at the same time we get to know ourselves better.

Other prominent emotions we feel are guilt, anger and shame. Guilt is a tension between our ego self and our higher self. We feel guilty for giving into fear and not forgiving ourselves and others. Not forgiving equals not loving. People who are loving and accepting have less guilt, for they choose love over fear. In general, it is safe to say that all the "negative" emotions have to deal with a deep sense that we are missing something in our life due to a misperception, misunderstanding or denying love.

People who manage to get in touch with their higher self, their love-based self, tend to invoke envy in those who still operate on ego and fear. Envy may occur when a fear-based person feels that another person acts from a truthful principle, such as love, that he still chooses to deny. Envious people act as if you took something from them. When you act on higher-self love it appears that you have access to some profound commodity and those who are not choosing to do the same may envy your ability / choice to connect with love! It is because they identify so deeply with the fear / pain body that they go to great lengths to maintain it.

Misplaced Anger

When we meet people who for no apparent reason resist us and act defiantly - it could be that we trigger in them feelings of unresolved anger. It could be that their pain level is high and even a small trigger can unleash it. I once had a phone call on a Sunday afternoon from a 19-year-old prospective client who was inquiring about my services. When I asked her why she wanted to have holistic reflexology sessions, she mentioned a foot pain due to an injury.

Before I could respond, she went on to describe how the foot pain radiated to her pelvis. She did not stop there. She added that the pain was also in her private parts and went on to describe some unsuccessful healing experience she had in the past. Her speech was scattered and unfocused. I wasn't sure how to respond. When I said that in my observation many body ailments are often mind-body and perhaps emotionally based she angrily dismissed my statement by saying that her "thing" was not emotional. I said that she may be right, yet in my experience more often than not there is not a separation between mind-body. At that point she sounded increasingly defiant so I just asked for her phone number so that I could try to work things out with her at a later time. Her tone got angrier and I said we shall talk again soon. After we hung up I felt that her tone was so strong that I was somewhat concerned.

Something just wasn't right. Soon after, I found a voice message on my phone from her. She said: "Don't call me back, you just don't understand! You don't even know what's going on!" When I reflected on the whole thing, I realized that she had some built up pain and that all it took was to say one wrong word for her to set off her anger. I think that my bringing up the emotional concept of her physical pain was a trigger.

I thought that she was not listening to anything I said to her. I felt that what happened was "filtration" of sorts - to make sure that we were ready to work together. When I reflected on the other things she said, I realized there were clearly some sexual issues going on. Maybe she expected me to guess, but she blocked the holistic approach. The final hint that something was just not right was in the end of our conversation. She mentioned that she had had two reflexology sessions with a lady and that it all went well until the lady started "to touch beyond the feet" – probably working on the calves. My feeling was that the "foot pain" is a link to some unresolved pain in her female reproductive parts. While there is no reason not to see a client who resists metaphysical counseling, I was still uncomfortable with her attitude from the get go. She may have insinuated to sexual abuse. The second phone call was the answer. We were not ready for each other. Her approach was that of misplaced anger – I did no harm to her but nevertheless her anger needed an outlet.

Remember the saying:
The teacher appears when the student is ready.

Everything has time and place. The way she rejected my suggestion of "mind-body" connection and was so unclear about her true needs meant that, for now, it's better to wait. It is frustrating to face pain mixed with so much resistance that it won't allow for intervention. But this is a part of the journey. Maybe I had to learn to be more cautious with the mind-body idea. After thinking about it, I realized that her emotional pain was probably larger than her physical pain. When we face an emotional pain, we are also called on a truth. The Italians have a saying "the truth will hurt you, yet it will liberate you." We can free ourselves from pain on all levels by delving into its source and facing our worst fears.

When people feel helpless and defeated, they sometimes grasp for energy by trying to feed on others. When I was a Sunday school teacher I encountered the "yes, but" students. No matter what reply you give to their question, there was always a "yes, but." There is also the "eternal questioner" or "professional asker": Asking questions over and over barely allowing you to respond. All these patterns may reflect an attempt to grasp for some perceived lost energy that was deprived, or stolen, or otherwise not available to that person in the past. Some call this pattern "control drama." Their behavior feeds on the pain / fear body and seeks to find a match in an equivalent person or situation.

When we call people on their control drama they tend to get upset. Calling someone on their drama means they may have to look inside and process their feelings - when it can be difficult and painful thing to do. Allowing such drama, without becoming reactive, can by itself be healing - for it leaves the "attacker" with nobody "attacked." When we chose not to react we shift from reactive to proactive behavior and we become more present and liberated. Reactive behavior is ego based, "push button" style of conduct. It is ego galore - the density of the mind and its many short circuits. We don't grow in this fear. We are just recycling the same misperceptions over and over.

To step out of this vicious cycle is to truly move forward and grow. In a proactive mode, we silently count to ten, take a deep breath and take action based on a choice. Without a choice, we're on automatic pilot. When we count to ten and observe our reaction to a situation, we then see that we can still make a choice on how to proceed - it's a victory of the love-based higher self. It's like the saying "It is better to be wise than to be right." For example, when someone cuts you off while driving on the highway, you can choose a positive response. The best response is the one that will not adversely affect your balance and not engage you in a reactive behavior. Maintaining our own equilibrium is about how everything around us affects and is affected by us.

Pauline's Story

I once had a client, "Pauline" who suffered from severe constipation for many years, but was uncomfortable discussing her bowel movements, since she thought it was very personal. Towards the end of the session she started to cry, but she said she was OK. In order to clarify and focus her feelings, I asked her to select a card from an inspirational card deck I had. She picked the card that said "Give up resistance for it prolongs your pain." When she saw this card she became very angry and threw it back on the table. She said all she wanted was to be in peace and she was hoping for a card that would discuss peace and not resistance. On a later date she agreed that the message was correct, that she could not attain peace without giving up her resistance. In her case, her resistance was probably causing her constipation. The messages inherent in cards we draw, and symbols we see, can be powerful. We can always use a reminder from the universe. Whether these reminders come from cards, from symbols or from our subconscious is a matter of observation.

We Are What We Eat

What is certain is that the more in tune we are, the more "random" messages we get. These messages are strikingly accurate. I think messages can come from many directions. I once got a mailing request from a fundraising organization to help benefit baby cows that were being abused in the veal industry. I opened the envelope and saw pictures of calves sitting in their feces and urine, tied by their neck to a 22 inch cell that didn't even allow them to turn around. I was reading with exceeding discomfort. Somehow I felt sad and helpless.

The letter said that they are laced with antibiotics and deprived of water to force them to drink the medical formula that will ensure their meat has the right pink color. They are kept in darkness so they don't try to escape by banging against the walls of their cells. It said they only saw their mothers for a few hours after birth, causing birth trauma. I thought how this situation resembled many people's lives - constrained, poisoned, traumatized and helpless. I was wondering why this abuse hit me so hard since I am not even a vegetarian. I concluded that these animals deserved the basic humane conditions of life, regardless of their impending slaughter. If we treated our pets this way we could be in jail.

The food we eat has a frequency.

The feeling of despair in any living organism has a frequency. These frequencies are the sum of the various energies to which it was exposed. The more clean and lucid we are the more we are able to feel these frequencies. For example, you can't expect a poisoned and traumatized person to be in tune with the same substance that intoxicates him or her. It is only by cleaning and purifying the body that we can start feeling these frequencies.

I wrote a check that day for the calf protection charity. The next day, out of the blue, a friend sent me a message about a dairy cause and the abuse of cows in the controversial dairy industry. He went on to describe the milk production industry, the damages of milk consumption to humans and the public's lack of education on the subject. Consequently, the letter mentioned the poor calves and how they are cheated out of their milk which is instead used for human consumption. In other words, most of the milk we are consuming was taken from young calves - which instead received the horrible pharmaceutical drink and are treated from the beginning of their lives as a product and not a living organism.

I was stunned by the coincidence of the arrival of the two letters. They both dealt with almost the same topic. I am constantly amazed by how we are living in such serendipity. I was contemplating this situation in order to see the relativity of it to my life and to the lives of all humanity. Our culture still allows for cruelty and abuse, in this example, by the heavily lobbied meat and dairy industries. Everything we come in contact with reflects in our frequency. There are better ways to raise and consume the meat we eat that creates less suffering and raises, not lowers frequency.

109

Many aware farmers are now humanely raising livestock. They use more free-range, organic and sustainable farming methods. Seek them out; make that choice for yourself, for the animals and for our world.

With generous donations, many organizations are working around the clock to resolve and bring these sad stories of abuse to our awareness. We can rectify and remedy abusive situations with a more holistic approach that requires only one thing - action toward reducing suffering in the world. To reduce suffering means to reduce the collective pain we all carry. Since no separation exists in the Universe, our collective pain body can only be decreased by reducing world-wide suffering. There is no escape from the consequences unless there is improvement. In other words, we can never be separated from that which is all around us and from that which we are part of.

One would hope that in such a technologically advanced world that we would not allow for cruelty and abuse. Advancing technology does not automatically invoke compassion. Technology is mind-based. Only when technology is harnessed, and aligned with the heart, can we see progress. Heart-based living is a remedy for fear and pain, starting within each and every one of us and then projecting it outside. Never wonder, "What difference can just one person make, anyway?" The Universe is always in tune with our thoughts. We are here to perform the rectification of this world. This world is given to us to heal it as we heal ourselves. Every small step is valid. Any thought, intention, or deed has the power to destroy or heal. The choice is ours.

Becoming More Aware

What does it mean to be more aware? It means to aspire to own all our characteristics and to be responsible for living a

110

truthful life. This is only possible if we are able to see ourselves through our ego self - the pain / fear body, our perceptions, our minds. To be aware means to acknowledge that we have an ego and that it feeds on pain. Only through awareness can we radiate our true self and attract more light into our life. Ultimately, our interactions dwell on the recognition of light in others. Be aware of your initial gut feelings when you meet people. There is a surface level of being that is affected by our immediate moods and a deeper, more constant level of being that relates directly to our higher consciousness. Ideally, in our interactions, by recognizing light in others and intending to uplift and dissolve any perceived pain we see in them, we increase the level of light present in us. The only way to attract light and love is to give it freely.

The ego body, with its pain identification, believes that love is a limited commodity. Beyond this consciousness lies the eternal truth that all and everything is love. Therefore, ego misperceives love. Fear is the resistance and denial of love. The reason so many people sink in the "convenience" of pain and depression is that it allows them to avoid responsibility. Feelings of guilt and self reproach feed the pain and the need to seek negativity, to justify their paralysis. The word "depression" comes from Latin "deprimo" - to press down. The question arises, what is it that we press down? To put it under one umbrella, we press down our "shadow."

The shadow is everything we choose not to see - all the aspects of reality that we consciously avoid seeing or to which we are unconsciously blind. As we refuse owning our shadow we will seek to project it outside us, onto others. It's as if our shadow will always try to come to the surface somehow. We will find people and /or circumstances to project on. We will be sensitive about one topic, yet blunt and callous about another. We may even seek in others the blemishes that we carry. By recognizing in others what we refuse to see in ourselves, we become more and more aware of that which we refuse to see.

**The more we see compassion, love and other fine qualities
outside of ourselves,
the more we actually project those positive aspects.**

Ultimately, the more we flow with the higher vibrations of our manifested life, the more we materialize and manifest people, places and circumstances that correspond to our output. The Universe can remind us that we are on the right track by subtle events of an apparent "random" nature. However, since "random" cannot exist in a world where everything is interconnected, we can accept all coincidences as messages from the Universe - messages that affirm that we are in the right place, doing the right thing, at the right time!

As we shift from ego-based behavior to real self or higher awareness, our need to speak "ego language" decreases. At first, we may realize that some people resist our shift, as if they are threatened by it. This is the work of their ego. Ego is a contractive entity and anything expansive threatens it. Identification with love and light is all inclusive, as it seeks to put all phenomena in the context of oneness. This all inclusiveness is foreign to the ego, because ego seeks to be exclusive and attempts to separate us through pain. It is not uncommon to feel the need to move on and leave behind friends, family and associates who resist our growth by wanting to connect through our ego consciousness. It is OK to move on and there is no judgment, just flow. As we let go of those who resonate with us less and less they in turn stand a chance to grow, as their density may loosen up and gradually allow for more reflection and connectedness. To lessen ego is to defy gravity.

When someone tries to invoke your ego self by provoking you, breathe deeply. Breathing makes you feel lighter. It helps to defy gravity. Then, see if you can feel the pain that they are trying to project on you as a faulty attempt to reduce their own pain. There is nothing malicious about them; it is an unconscious operation on their part to try and lighten up their heavy load. Breathe and let light go through you to them. Only respond if you feel the presence of light. If you get reactive you fall into the ego trap and thus contribute to the continuation of suffering. When you respond from light, you allow healing to take place. Even the density of the toughest egos respond to light and, like water tapping on stone, ultimately it can reshape it. It is only our acceptance of the "is-ness" of things, beyond good and bad that will allow us to bring more light to the world. As we do, our ego resistance dissolves and we start observing others with more acceptance and compassion, without being threatened by their choices. It is ultimately our choice to decide what feeds us and what doesn't. As we focus on what *is*, and invite more awareness to that which it *is*, we become one with universal light and wisdom.

As a part of becoming a being that channels light, we need to be more mindful of our heightened frequency. The words we say, the focus we have, the beauty and wonder we notice - are a part of this heightened frequency. Important factors in our growth are compassion to all life, responsibility to nature and its resources and investing in our "energy bank account" – the invisible account we have with the bank of the Universe. Getting to know ourselves, what unifies us and what distinguishes us is important. What are your challenges and what are your gifts? These are all important. As Emerson said, every heart vibrates to its own chord.

Ultimately, we heighten our frequency by elevating our soul connection and reducing our level of ego identification. Contemplation and soft breathing are great tools. We know we've moved in the right direction when we can handle "empty" moments without the need to create distraction. In the stillness there are glimpses into the "is-ness" of existence. That's when we tap into the unified breathing of all things.

113

Chapter Twelve:
Energetic Messages from the Soul

The Human Energy Fields

Most belief systems and spiritual orders support the theory that we are more than simply the physical body in which we exist. In fact, our bodies are merely one aspect of our lives and as an onion is composed of many layers, so is our existence.

The modern spiritual scientist Dr. Rudolf Steiner classifies the human anatomy into four levels.
1. The Physical Body – the mechanical and biochemical components of the body.
2. The Ethereal Body – the life aura layer which immediately surrounds the physical body.
3. The Astral Body – the seat of the soul and its karmic manifestations in correlation to the cosmos and its influences.

4. The Spiritual Body – the true spiritual essence of the human being. The divine self.

Note: Do not worry if these terms seem confusing. As you are about to see, things seem more simple when we take a closer look at our connection with the universe.

The Human Soul

The soul is the eternal, timeless existence by which we are all surrounded. In between the soul and the body we find the ethereal body or what we think of as our aura, and our astral body which acts as the bridge or intermediary between our physical and spiritual existence. The human soul is a continuum that defies time and space. In other words, while our bodies may die, the soul remains eternal in its existence. It will carry in its resonance our life stories of past, present and perhaps future times. In a broader sense, we also carry the memories of all humanity that has gone before us. The ethereal fields are not only directly linked to the daily experiences we have, but also to astral / soul-based frequencies such as past life incarnations. Though the soul possesses memories and experiences from other lifetimes, the astral body is the soul version of our human existence and consciousness.

The Physical Body

First and foremost, our physical body is a part of the World of Forms. It is always a physical manifestation of a hidden reality. However, at this level, the body is just what it is – a shape, a form subjected to time, space and hence the laws of gravity.

116

The Ethereal Body

All life forms have a field of magnetism to them, sometimes called aura field. These electromagnetic forces are present in the physical body and are similar to the ethereal body. Although ethereal energies are not identical to electromagnetic forces they still seem to be affecting electromagnetic fields. An example of the existence of the ethereal body is when a person who lost a limb feels the sensation of the lost limb as if it were still there. Moreover, this limb may still show intact in the person's aura field.

This occurrence is also illustrated in Kirilian photography. Named for the Russian scientist Semyon Kirilian, it is a technique that uses high voltage electrical charges to create photographic images of plant, animal and human energy fields. In a famous Kirilian experiment, a leaf was photographed, then a piece of the leaf was removed and another photograph was taken. In the second photograph, the energy field still remained in the area that had been removed. The leaf remembered its full self in spite of the removal of its part.

All living things have an ethereal body. It is this body that distinguishes between that which is living and that which is not. There is a direct parallel between a strong ethereal body and life force. When the ethereal body is strong the physical body is vital. The ethereal body is a sort of energetic imprint of our most basic physical existence. Understanding the ethereal body as an energy field is important in recognizing the non-tangibility aspect of life.

**Understanding the notion that
there are energetic fields
inherent to our physical body
is a key in healing.**

In another famous experiment, plants were exposed to sounds of different emotional expressions - from angry yelling to the soothing whispering of loving thoughts. The plants responded to the different emotions and reflected them in their growth. This is a key revelation in the importance of affirmations and thoughts. Similar experiments have been done with water and its response to a range of emotional expression, with intriguing results. The assumption is that as the body is comprised mostly of water, our cellular response to various frequencies is greater than we know.

The Astral Body – Our Chakra System

In humans the astral body is the seat of the soul – the part of us which is comprised of our feelings, desires and emotions – stemming from our Karmic choices of reincarnation. Whereas the ethereal body imparts vitality, it is the astral body that imparts color and depth in our life. A major component of the astral teachings is the existence of seven energy centers, or Chakras. Each Chakra has its own characteristics and corresponds to an aspect of our being. The seven Chakras relate to the human existence and evolution. Because the Chakra system is the processing center for every aspect of our being, any energetic dysfunction can create disorders in the body, mind and spirit.

Each of the seven Chakras is an energetic connection to pure consciousness and Spirit. Each Chakra allows for the next one to unfold. It is said that the first three Chakras represent the ego, the fourth or heart Chakra is a center of love and a bridge to the higher Chakras, and Chakras five, six and seven represent our higher self. For further explanation see the Chakra Chart in Appendix X.

The Spiritual Body

If we are to accept eternity and re-incarnation, this is the part of each of us that is a spark of the divine. It is this from this form that we supposedly "fell from grace" – from the Spiritual World to the World of Forms (the physical reality). It is this realm that we aspire to reconnect with again; it is the one-ness, the pre-fragmentation form – the love and the wholeness that is the true reality beyond this all - the journey of rediscovering our true self.

The Alchemy of Spirituality

The notion of a connection between the human soul and a universal soul is deeply rooted in the tradition of alchemy. Alchemy is often seen as a primitive version of modern chemistry. In spite of the fact that it is widely down played today as just a mind-game practice, alchemy has profound roots in philosophies that recognize the inter-connectedness of all spheres, human nature and the Universe. Alchemical practice theorized that nature contains all the secrets of existence and by understanding it we can draw on the larger cosmos.

A famous teacher of this theory was Paracelsus, a medieval Swiss alchemist. He drew on the direct connection among man, nature and the cosmos as a gateway to the higher laws. In his *Doctrine of Signatures* he described how shapes of different plants corresponded to human health. This was a poetic observation of shapes as being universal, for example, a heart shaped leaf corresponds to the heart. In other words, nature and man are one and correspond to each other.

Paracelsus also connected the heavenly bodies, planets and stars to plants and minerals. Being a famed alchemist, Paracelsus thought of refining natural phenomena into subtle symbolism. This ability to draw on nature as connected to the human experience and the cosmos is highly poetic in that he claimed that all shapes and forms have similar meanings, wherever they are found. This perception of reality is pretty much on the continuum of the "as above, so below" paradigm as it endorses correspondence.

As modern science advanced it distanced itself from its metaphysical roots and developed a more linear paradigm whose belief was energy and matter did not truly connect. This split between energy and matter affected not only modern chemistry and science, but also the field of medicine and psychology. This is especially true in the case of psychiatry which draws on the medical model of the body as a mechanical entity. Some psychologists follow the Jungian approach of relating to the inner soul life of the person, but usually even they come short of the link between human existence and nature. Science truly alienated itself from nature and lost the symbolic and poetic connection that ties all phenomena. Speaking poetically, nature has a soul and this soul unifies all of nature's manifestations.

Tapping into the soul and frequency of nature
brings us more into alignment
with the frequency of the Universe.

In this regard, illness and disease stem from a misunderstanding, not only of us with ourselves, but also to the greater principles that govern the world of nature and the cosmos. One can ask: "What are the laws that surround me and how do I expose myself to them?" One possible answer would be that it takes personal observation and patience and a good start would be to relate to the world of symbolism (for example: animals, plants, astrology and dreams). The indigenous North American people were highly versed in observing animals and their relation to the human experience. Their medicine of totem animals saw a direct link between one's personal animal and one's well being.

120

The Shaman's Way

In ancient times a person who needed guidance would come before the elders. The elders had shamanic wisdom and knew the secrets of life. They experienced powerful visions and regarded their own healing abilities as a divine gift. In an elaborate ceremony, animal symbols were chosen and the shamans would counsel as to the meaning of the choices and provided the guidance needed to attain healing. The power animal is also called totem. Learn more about the Totem Animal Chart in Appendix XI.

In Native American Shamanism, as we connect to the power of an animal via omens, divination and sighting, we are asking to align ourselves with its complete power and harmonize with its essence. This connection with the animal world could also be done through dream analysis. Each animal has its own message and depending on how it appeared, the Shamans would decide what aspect of its symbolism is important. Another method is animal divination. They would take parts of different animals such as a wolf claw or a bear tooth and put them together in a basket or bowl. Then when an individual picked out one of these pieces it was representative of a symptom or trait the person carried. If the tooth or claw was selected upside down, it also held a meaning.

For example, if we selected the symbol of the Armadillo, a claw or scale from its armor, it would represent boundaries. It would mean we need to set our boundaries with others and own our experiences without being invaded. Armadillos heal the sense of being invaded by other people. Drawing an Armadillo symbol would call us to define our space and honor our personal time. It is also great medicine for when we feel we are being taken for granted. However, if we drew the Armadillo scale upside down or an Armadillo card in its reverse state the interpretation could be that we needed to be more vulnerable and open up to others, or that we need to stop hiding and open up our boundaries.

Another powerful practice is for the Shaman to symbolically connect with a sick person's chosen power animal and visualize it performing an exuberant dance because usually a sick person would most likely have a totem animal that was feeling lethargic. Upon the Shamans visualization the individual would oftentimes feel better. The Shaman identifies the medicine animal or totem by its attributes and connection to the sick person and affects change through his visualization. This is symbolic work and is a highly organic approach to healing; it draws on the belief that our spirit is nourished by an external energy source and that the animal totem is an archetypal bridge to that source.

Native American medicine is an example of interconnectedness between man and nature. I often discuss the theme of birds with any client who has experienced a recent loss of a family member. Sometimes they report that, in the first days after their loss, a bird suddenly appeared in their immediate vicinity and acted in an unusual manner, like staying on a tree branch the whole day. I recently had a client who lost her mom. I told her to watch for any unusual appearance of birds surrounding her. She called me the next day almost hysterical and told me that, while she was sitting on her patio overlooking a pond, a big crane flew by. The bird strangely tapped some plants with its feet and then flew away only to do it again and then disappeared. She said had never seen this bird before or after this occurrence.

She also remembered that immediately after the death while she was preparing funeral arrangements a crow was flying over her head. She said that as she was walking out of the funeral home, it flew down in an unusually low altitude and circled right above her head. It was basically following her. She remarked about it to her siblings, but they dismissed it. I'm not saying there's a definite explanation for this, but I do think that birds represent the air element, thus the spirit world.

The same connection we have with animals can be made with plants, minerals and the elements to include all of nature. It is only through complete harmony with nature that we can live in harmony and health and truly experience life by becoming fully ourselves. The ability to fully own ourselves in well-being and infinite potential is contingent on awakening the innate capacities of our souls. Our journey is a quest for wholeness based on the understanding that there exists an invisible dimension that is a part of our visible reality. These two dimensions are a part of the bigger picture, the one that goes beyond linear time and space.

Another fascinating connection between the human journey and nature is found in Bach flower remedies. Dr. Edward Bach's flower essences captured the wavelength of different plants and connected them to the human experience based on flowers being the soul of nature. By connecting with the frequency of the flowers we connect to nature's soul, thereby connecting to our own soul. In the case of the flower essence, one ingests their vibration and therefore aligns with their respective properties. In healing in general it is very important to possess a somewhat poetic view. Science is always important, yet the combination of science and art makes for a broader perception of reality.

In this regard planetary magnetic fields can be the explanation for astrology. The planets may not directly guide our life, yet it is worthwhile to understand their symbolic meaning. It is a universal symbolism that dates back to the creation of the world.

Determining our Destiny

Many events in our life may happen for some hidden reason. We may not always know what power guided them or even believe that such power even existed. Instead of stating your lack of belief, state your lack of knowledge. As soon as we proclaim our lack of knowing, the Universe immediately starts to teach us about it. Have you ever said to yourself "I just don't understand why such-and-such always happens" just to realize that as soon as you acknowledge that you don't know, the answer may start presenting itself? The Universe appreciates our honesty and as soon as we admit our lack of knowledge the Universe considers it a request to learn and soon enough to know.

Nothing determines our destiny more than our own thoughts and beliefs.

It is not so much our destiny that we need to work on as much as we need to work on our density. When we diffuse density we change our thoughts and belief systems. Density is always fear-based and to diffuse density is to release fear. Density and gravity go hand-in-hand and the air element, with its infinite potential, is only a force of gravity. The less gravity present, the more we allow the air element to soar and connect us with our true soul nature. The feet are incredible gateways to release gravity in that they are the densest part of the body. Rub your feet often, for the increase in circulation helps to ground your body and soul. Simply take some natural lotion and rub your feet any way that feels good.

The ancient Greeks had a mantra for self improvement. "Know thyself." The idea is that by looking within, all the answers are present. Very often when we are asked to look within, our breathing becomes shallow. That's because we are looking through the lens of perception and conditional love. It is this very perception and conditional love that causes our suffering. Changing this perception will allow us to look within and see ourselves in a new light."Know thyself" also draws on knowledge as opposed to perception. As we saw before knowing is not the same as believing. Knowing is truth and believing may be a perceived truth.

Affirmations may not work when we are affirming statements that we don't believe in. Yet, believing may stand in the way between us and our knowledge. Affirmations are a bridge to our inner knowledge that replaces faulty beliefs. How can we affirm something while we believe the opposite? It is like building a bridge. The more we affirm the more solid is the bridge. Our beliefs may hold us powerless and they may stand for our biggest fear - the fear that we are actually powerful people with infinite resources ahead of us. Just like in breathing we observe expansion and contraction - so is the mechanism of the human experience. It is sometimes the fear of expansion that pushes us to contract, but the eternal dance of life entails that true movement is only possible through the polarities of expansion and contraction.

Above all, our journey demands that we re-align and change our beliefs, thought patterns and perceptions. Mind / body medicine draws heavily on changing core beliefs and perceptions, some of which are not even conscious. See Examples of Mind / Body Connections in Appendix XIV. Our core beliefs and thoughts are like a muscle, sometimes they stretch out and sometimes they flex back. For example, it's not enough to attend a lifestyle workshop during which we had stretched ourselves and declare that we are permanently healed. When we do this we oftentimes have a contractive or flexing reaction. Healing can be like a dance where we move two steps forward and one step backward. Allow yourself to be patient with the step backwards, relax with the flexion. It is not a failure; it is simply the natural waning of the movement of nature. The need to step backward is present in the ebb of the ocean waves and the exhale of the breathing process.

Biorhythms

A rhythm is a vibration pattern (often represented through sound or movement) that repeats in a consistent frequency for a certain period of time. The first rhythm we are exposed to is our mother's heartbeat. Biorhythms are the sum of all the rhythmical cycles in our lives. We always live under the laws of biorhythm, e.g. sleep/wake. They are present in our bodies and in the Universe and are essential in understanding the powers that surround us. They are the movement between polarities which allows us to be active and then regain energy through rest.

The human body has three different biorhythms:
1. Physical – 23 days
2. Emotional – 28 days
3. Mental – 33 days

We live in a repeated cycle of 23, 28 or 33 days in which we tend to go into lows and highs within the cycle. The organ that is in charge of biorhythm is the pineal gland. The pineal gland is a part of the brain and is located in the center of the skull right behind the eyebrows. It is shaped like a pine nut and is considered the "third eye" or the intuition center. The attributes of the pineal gland include a vision beyond vision – intuition. There is also the 24 hour cycle of body organs – each organ has its own peak and down time.

The pineal gland became very popular in the 1990's with the discovery of melatonin, which is a hormone it secretes. Melatonin affects the biorhythm patterns of sleeping and waking - allowing for better sleep – and generally diminishes in people over age 40. It is also a very powerful antioxidant. The pineal gland in its optimal function is essential for well being, in that the body is in balance with the cycles of life. We seldom think of our organs as needing to rest. We may assume that they are there for us twenty four hours a day, seven days a week. The truth is that good health is only available when the components of our body get their replenishing time so they can properly function.

Getting sunlight to the forehead can be essential for the pineal gland as it also affects our moods. In face reading, the area of the third eye is the area of the liver. Since the liver is responsible for the emotional processing of anger it is safe to say that the more clogged the liver is the more energetically clogged the third eye

area would be, therefore anger clogs our intuition.
For more information, see the Biorhythm Chart in Appendix XII.

On Karma, Life and Trauma

There is as a misconception that Karma is a "punishment."
We may believe we are suffering because it is our "Karma." In
fact, this is far from being true. Karma is a natural law. In the
realm of interconnectedness past incarnations can manifest as
present desires, thoughts, actions and beliefs. Pluto symbolizes
karmic residues that we are trying to eliminate. Astrologically,
Pluto was always connected to the "underworld." In Greek
mythology Pluto was symbolic of Hades and Dionysus. Dionysus
was the underworld god of wine consumption. His link to Pluto
can explain why we often act on impulses and compulsions. Being
under the influence of alcohol steers up all hidden patterns in us
and invokes our own hidden or underworld side.

As we observed, alcohol is a fermented love substitute for
true love and as many of our unresolved issues stem from some
disturbed connection to love, it takes a state of "fermented love" to
release patterns connected to it. Similar attracts similar. This
explains why under alcoholic influence so many of our hidden
patterns come out - we reveal our hidden desires and unresolved
conflicts. Fermented love can never equal true love. For it
represents stagnation.

Real love flows freely.
When we hold it, ignore it or otherwise stop its flow
– it becomes stale –
a rancid version of the real thing.

Let's take a look at addiction from the astrological

viewpoint. In astrology, our sun sign reveals what we are assimilating and it reflects our innermost self. Pluto on the other hand shows what we are eliminating in our growth process. Addiction falls greatly under the Pluto category. Another way to understand how we move between assimilation and elimination is to take a look at the laws of gravity. Karma is similar to gravity in that we fall under its laws unless we branch away and defy it. To defy gravity, which is the weight of our physical existence, means to dissolve the patterns that set us off emotionally and mentally. Fear is the ultimate karma-gravity force, whereas love is the power to undo fear and karma and defy the gravity in our lives.

The Script Game

Many people report traumatic events that shaped their lives in one way or another. In times of stress, these events and/or the pattern inherent within them, return to the surface as fear and anxiety. To address the mind's tendency to dwell on more stress while under stress we can play The Script Game. In this game, you are asked to look at a major trauma or a life event that you consider a source of great stress. It can be anything from childhood trauma of loss to a death in the family or difficult events of any sort. Now describe the true event without changing its details. Pretend that all this is happening in a movie and you are merely watching a scene from a movie. Let's call this real story "Script A."

Now you are asked to become the editor of the movie of your life. As editor you have the ability to substitute any scene from the movie with any other possible segment - without tossing or destroying the initial scene. Invent a new script for a new scene which will be a substitute for Script A. In this new script, called Script B, go back to the difficult event and substitute it with a joyful, fulfilling and compassionate sequence instead. This is done without ever canceling the existence of Script A. It is simply utilizing your ability to choose an option.

The mind is a powerful tool. Since the past has truly passed, all that is left from the real Script A is what we make of it now. Based on our perceptions, presenting Script B allows for a healing dialogue between the scripts to a point that Script A is not denied, yet allows for script B to become a viable imprint, an alternative story that develops its own frequency and thus is energetically viable. It is as if Script B is a bridge over Script A - a safe path over a turbulent river. It is safer to cross any bridge from a point of strength. This is not necessarily a mind game; it is a true reinventing of events leading to a change of perception which reduces unnecessary suffering. I have witnessed dysfunction and pain connected to people's true trying life events and The Script Game is a creative technique that allows for crutches to be used to cross a difficult segment of the road.

Take a moment now and recall a real event and try your hand at it following the examples below.

Script A to Script B Transformation

First Example:	
Script A: The Real Event	As a child, you come home from school. It's your birthday. Your mom greets you with yelling. Later when your dad comes home from work he drinks heavily and acts mean. Nobody seemed to remember it was your birthday. You go to bed disappointed and sad.
Script B: Remaking of The Event	You come home from school. It's your birthday. There is nobody home, but when you open the fridge you see your surprise birthday cake. Shortly after, your parents arrive and set a fabulous birthday dinner for you. You proudly

	blow out all the candles on the cake. While slicing the cake you feel so happy, loved and appreciated. All is well.

Second Example:	
Script A: The Real Event	Your father left home in your early childhood. You don't remember him. You were raised by several step fathers, some were angry and abusive. You have sad memories from these situations in which you felt repeatedly unloved.
Script B: Remaking of the Event	You receive a beautiful letter, as a child, from your father whom you don't remember. It explains why he had to leave and reassures you that he always loved you and he regrets his shortcomings. He is apologetic for all the suffering that followed and he says you were always in his prayers. He tells you his leaving had nothing to do with you and if he had to do it over again he would surely try to be more responsible and thoughtful. You accept his apology in the sense that you understand it wasn't about you. You feel a relief and you are more open to accept the past as a chain of misunderstandings and shortcomings not intended to hurt you personally.

**The truth is that our life events can always be seen as karmic,
a choice of some sort,
that goes far beyond good or bad.**

In this respect, karma is only as real as we allow it to be.
By gradually shifting to a love-based life we can re-merge with the

powers that connect us to our higher self. By doing so, we are defying repeated karmic patterns or certain events and tendencies in our life. It is when we don't change the karmic patterns that we make our lives difficult and unbearable. With a love-based consciousness we can defy gravity in the sense that karma is the weight of dense energetic residue.

Life always brings challenges to deal with and often we become overwhelmed. Instead, we can choose to observe the events of our lives with objectivity and a clear perspective. Although it may likely result in feeling some sadness or agitation, keep your attention on distancing yourself from your life, as if you were watching a movie. In this state we not only can see a broader angle of our life, but through affirmations and re-scripting, we also manipulate the flow of our life's events and plant the seeds of favorable outcomes. This is how you heal along your spiritual path.

~Part III: INTEGRATION:
All One & All Right~

Chapter Thirteen:
Manifest Healing

What Impairs Our Healing Process

Much is said about healing and why people don't heal. Often after taking a workshop or a seminar we feel elated and knowledgeable. Then we face a downfall shortly thereafter when we have to deal with our same frustrations and issues again. We may have worked on changing our minds about our issues, but our emotional body governs our ultimate thinking and decision making. It is not easy to address the emotional body through mental channels. We can assume that all is well now, but we may not have erased the unresolved issues that we carry within us.

Our cells carry cellular memory which is the sum of our experiences on all levels, and through a very elaborate and intentional process even our cellular memories can be altered. When done properly, affirmations have proven to be quite powerful and penetrating. We understand that what we project we therefore receive. Then, why do we still deal with the same stress factors after we have whole-heartedly affirmed that we no longer need them in our life? The answer is complex and the secret is in the present moment. Remember that healing is a process.

Affirmations not only work on a mental level, they need to connect with the deeper levels of our emotional and spiritual selves, mostly through the subconscious, but how much access do we truly have to our subconscious? Though our subconscious mind mysteriously governs us, it isn't always easily accessible. Tapping into the power of affirmation is essential to tapping into the basic emotions such as joy, anger, grief and fear.

We all came into this world with agreements regarding the lessons and work we need to accomplish in this lifetime. These agreements entail experiences that extend beyond what we call good or bad because it all serves the bigger picture of why we are here in the first place. It is only our ego mind that makes judgments of good or bad. The ego mind avoids pain like the plague, yet in its own convoluted way it keeps inflicting pain. By avoiding pain, our higher self may not always be able to provide us with the right answers to our life questions. Courage is essential for growth, for it allows us to go into the dark chambers of our soul without feeling that we will perish by doing so. The gravity of the subconscious is so strong that it affects our life circumstances. In a way, our subconscious mind corresponds to all that we refuse to see, namely our shadow.

We truly project our subconscious onto our daily life.

Examine your friends, the events of your day, what made you happy or sad, satisfied or disappointed. All these events have to do with our core beliefs about who we are and why we are here. It is also important to reduce as many stress factors as possible from our life. Do you have food sensitivity and/or allergy? Do you feel weak after eating certain food? Eliminating toxins from our

136

diet, as well as our emotional life, will prove miraculous in that it will eliminate stress and allow for better contact with our subconscious mind. It is hard to listen to and heal ourselves when our body is under attack. Always seek what feeds your well being and examine what doesn't.

Think of two important people in your life. Put their names on a piece of paper and write down three things that you appreciate about each of them. Now add your name to the list and write three things down that you appreciate about yourself. Take a deep breath and see how it feels to validate yourself. Do you own it or do you feel uncomfortable? If you don't feel comfortable, try to relate to the feeling. Is it because you're not allowed to, or supposed to appreciate yourself and, if so, by whose decree? The only person who controls your destiny is you. One of the interesting things about the ego is that while it supposedly seeks pleasure, many people do not truly know how to receive pleasure. Physically, this malady often manifests itself in low back pain and problems with the 4th and 5th lumbar of the spine (L4 & L5).

The ego may resist a pleasure that nurtures us profoundly and instead will tend to thrive on quick fixes such as addictions. This could be partially because true nurturing can only come from a true connection with us and our ego, and ego does not thrive on self knowledge. For example, someone can enjoy a massage, but when the practitioner discusses deeper themes in the person's life, he or she may be more resistant to cooperate. Through mind-body connection, wellbeing can be achieved whether through body work, nutrition, affirmations and/or any other methodology that establishes the connection between us and our world. The more we feel connected the healthier and happier we may be. Many ailments on all levels stem from poor connections.

The ego thrives on attack and it often responds to the notion of being attacked and therefore attacks back. In a true emancipated self where the higher self takes the lead, we can never be attacked - no matter what. Being attacked is a perception and it takes an illusionary mind to accept that we can be attacked. We are not talking about life and death situations such as violent crimes. Even then, connecting to our higher self may affect the outcome as the ego thrives on fear and the higher self projects a different wavelength that is more inclusive AND understanding. Everybody has the capacity to respond to this wavelength and this is the key to undoing suffering.

Monitoring what we feel "in this very moment" and how we are breathing "in this very moment" is a key to how our thought patterns work and how we can choose to shift them in a favorable direction. It is very important to be in touch with our subconscious and bring it forward to our conscious mind. I always maintained that true happiness is possible by merging conscious and subconscious so that we may live a more unified life. Any time you feel unhappy or stressed, catch yourself in the moment and observe your thoughts and feelings—and how you are breathing—and from where they originate. They all may very likely go back to a fear of some sort. As you acknowledge this fear and make your way out of it by choosing a positive affirmation, you gain a precious key to undo the moment in a different way and to unfold it in a favorable manner. A positive affirmation would be created by stating your intended future outcome as if it were already true now. It is important to repeat or read our affirmations frequently. This activity aids in changing our thinking and our reality. This is a process that can take many attempts. It is ongoing work, but gradually we find that the ego governs our life less and less and a higher self presence affects our life more and more.

Affirmations can greatly affect the metaphysical "stitch" points where body and energy meet and become one. When you feel stuck or unable to even start the healing process, remind yourself that you are responding to the presence of light. We can deliberately invite light from the Universe to come into our life or into a particular situation. In our daily dealings, we often respond with ego and the fight or flight mechanism. When facing a difficult situation, pause and allow for the light to come in and then rethink the situation from a new angle. Light is an infinite power and is directly connected to our ability to circulate joy in our life. Just like love and light are the only true states of the Universe so is joy the only true state in the human experience. All situations that don't correspond to joy are stemming in misunderstandings and ego interference. The infinity of love, light and joy is identical to the abundance of the Universe.

Learning really matters. Every learning experience we have comes from the vast ocean of knowing. One can argue that all knowledge is within us and that we are merely rediscovering that which we already know. All of our life experiences are threads that add up to the fabric of our true self. Knowledge is a deposit in our soul bank account. Although we may be born with all knowledge, we go through the process of rediscovering because we have to "learn / earn" each lesson. Otherwise we would not even need to be here. Regaining knowledge is so powerful. Often times the Universe provides us with what we need at "random." Opening a book and looking at a random page, turning on the T.V. and getting a message that connects us to our knowing. Do not discount these apparent coincidences; be aware of them for these are messages from our subconscious to our consciousness.

There is no such thing as random.

Always learn by experience - yours and others. Not only can others teach us by observing them, but we can also tap into the spirit or energy of deceased people in order to align ourselves with their greatness. I enjoy reading a century old author who did just that - sitting in imaginary conferences with his favorite figures. He would surround himself with figures from the political world, finance or literature and then present his current issues while consulting with his imaginary figures. This is a wonderfully creative way to tap into the vastness of the ocean of all knowledge.

139

How to Manifest the Best

The paradigm of the glass appearing to be half full or half empty is basic. Beyond all its meaning, there are people who are naturally more or less optimistic. Personal traits cannot be ignored and it's impossible to put us on the scale with each other. However when looking at "optimists" we can see a connection with optimism, courage, intuition, self reliance and sweetness. In pessimism we can see defeatism, linear thinking (intellectual / rational) and bitterness. It is safe to say that being able to see love in its many forms is a key to self transformation - becoming more optimistic and self reliant. The more we see love, the more we connect to the Universe and allow it to flow.

It is not an accident that in many religions God is referred to as a father. There is often a connection between a severed relationship to a parent figure in childhood and being cut off from the spiritual world. Often people feel cut off spiritually because their primary relationship, namely their connection to their parents--was not well established. Many fathers were too busy working or otherwise not (physically or emotionally) available. This could have contributed to a sense of disconnection from the father figure. Consequently, this became a "betrayal" of sorts. This betrayal by a father figure contributes to mistrust of the divine as well as all spirituality. Some people turn to spirituality to compensate for the lack of a supportive father figure. Others act on the betrayal and become alienated from the world of spirituality and by this may lose the essence of a full life, a life that is the interconnection between energy and matter.

Faith is the foundation of a spiritual life. Having faith may be easier for some people to achieve because they know how to use it as a replacement for fear, whereas others may feel alienated from the spiritual world. When this happens we may fear spirituality and develop mistrust in the process of life. The more faith we have the less fear can exist. Faith is "knowingness" just like a child knows things - it defies rationalism. Faith makes us present while fear keeps us in "fear time" which is anything but the present moment. Keep in mind that sometimes even faith is fear based. Do not confuse faith with dogma.

Inhale Faith, Exhale Fear

Here's a great Breathing Exercise: As you inhale think "love and light" and as you exhale think "fear and ego." Do this for a minute or so and see how it feels. Once you have released the fear, keep the following in mind.
1. Always hope for the best.
2. Always shoot for the best.
3. Always expect the best.
4. Always accept the outcome with peace.

The more *in harmony* we are with ourselves the more harmony unfolds in our life. Every time an unpleasant event happens to you, ask yourself how much in harmony you've been. People, events and circumstances can only happen in line with what we have put out to the Universe. In other words, there are no accidents or coincidences surrounding the people we meet and the places we go. The Universe only responds to the messages we send its way. It's like an echo, a mirror. Send and give love and you manifest love. Be generous in life and life will be generous with you. To receive more of that which you want, always give more of just that. Give freely of that which you desire. Give and you shall receive.

Chapter Fourteen:
Become Proactive

The Art of Being Proactive

In our daily dealings, events often happen so fast that we don't always have the chance to act from our full knowledge and wisdom. The more chaotic the events are, the more chance we will act from our reactive mode, the ego. To act proactively, being a step ahead as events unfold is a task. The more proactive we are, the more we respond to the laws of cause and effect. We can remain in the moment by not losing touch with our breathing. Breathing in the light and love of the universe and breathing out the fear and anger of the ego.

Being proactive is when we allow the light to come through. It puts us in an open mode of compassion and acceptance, forgiveness and wisdom. By being proactive we lessen suffering. Being proactive also means acting from our higher self. For example, someone cuts you off while driving, you look at them and not only do they not wave or apologize, they make a profane gesture. Now you have been violated and insulted. But in a proactive mode you can see that we are all interconnected and the other person is clearly attached to his / her ego therefore they are suffering. Their attempt to inflict more pain on you is a faulty attempt to reduce it in them.

We have the choice to engage or disengage. We can choose to smile, wave or just quietly forgive that person. The more we are able to actually let go of the need to engage in other people's pain and drama, the freer and lighter we can be. In fact, the more we rejoice in others' abundance and good fortune, the happier we can become. See all the events in your life as tests of the Universe that are directed to you. When we respond from the light and not from our ego – we score a definite A+. When our day begins, we can make a commitment to act from the light in a loving way to ourselves and others. At the end of the day, ask yourself how you responded from the light today. As an affirmation, make a list of how kind you were to yourself and others today. As we respond more and more with love and kindness our life becomes filled with more and more love and kindness. Acknowledge everything as coming from the light, even the most trying and difficult events.

Affirm:
Today I chose to love myself and others
- all is well in my life.

When we choose to live a love-based life we are called to surrender all control and allow Spirit to guide us. Surrendering is acknowledging the ego's illusionary nature. Although when we surrender our ego we may feel empty and void. That is when we must sit with the feeling of emptiness. It is in this place of emptiness that our higher self has a chance to manifest into our consciousness. Our higher self is always there and waiting. Trust the Universe in delivering it and always have faith in the journey.

All experiences are here to teach us an important lesson. The lesson always has do to with how we truly love ourselves and the world and how much we see the overall interconnectedness that surrounds us with an invisible thread of life and wonder, beyond judgment and fear. This is the realm of our higher self - the rest is an illusion. All our choices reflect the level of our commitment to our joy and self actualization.

Now is the time to affirm:
I am a beautiful being worthy of love.
I give and receive love freely.

One of the most common confusions about love is sex. How can sex be so bad if it's between two consenting adults? Social convention talks about the Ten Commandments and refraining from adultery. While this may be a great guideline, it says nothing of not rejoicing in our sexuality! It is not our job to judge others - we have enough work to do on our own. Sex can be a beautiful thing, an exchange of love and energy. It also governs the second Chakra - responsible for money and creativity. When we stifle our sexuality, we stifle channels of creativity and prosperity. Rather than stifling our sexual drive, we can *transmute* it.

Transmutation means taking energy from one level and shifting it to another level. Repressing is like putting a stone over the well and blocking access to it. William Blake, the English poet implied that energy repressed breeds pestilence. Do not repress – transmute! One way to transmute sexual energy is to live creatively. We are creative and sexy when we wear vibrant colors and have a coordinated style. The colors in our house, the food we eat, they can all be sexy. Sexy means full of life force. We can choose to have "sexy" thoughts. Every thought that is aligned with the infinite vibrant nature of the Universe is sexy. Sexy simply means to be in line with and receptive to universal vibration.

We Must Give to Get

Once when I was visiting India, I heard a beautiful tune playing from a house next to my guest house. I fell in love with it immediately. But it ended before I had the chance to find out its name. The next day while crossing a bridge in the yoga town of Rishikesh, I heard the same exact tune playing from a boom box. He spoke no English so I could not ask him about it. Finally, I went to the music shop where they sold cassette tapes. I tried to whistle the tune so that they could recognize it - to no avail. As a last resort, I asked them for a keyboard. They surely had an old keyboard at the back of the store. I played what little that I could remember from the tune and after playing it a few times they found a cassette tape. Bingo! It was it! It turns out that this tune was 15 years old and, even though the song was a bit old, for some reason I kept hearing it played everywhere as if it were a recent tune. The song was in Hindi so I asked for a translation, and it was something like "Love and mirrors are just about the same - both are bound to break."

Reflecting on the mirror quality of love, I thought about how relationships work. In a good relationship, we mirror each other. When we have a conflict in a relationship, it is often because we are trying to change the other person. Our thoughts and intentions focus on fixing them. Although it seems that in this process we are dealing with the other, we never are truly working on the other person per se. Only they can work on themselves. Even when we get upset and tell them how they should be or not be, we are actually working on ourselves – unbeknownst to us. Hopefully, the reality of the other person is close enough to the picture of the mate we have in mind. This can help to keep the focus on our own work and not feeling the need to work on them. By mirroring the best in each other we have a chance to grow.

We don't really live well until we act on service. Don't wait until all your soul issues are resolved to start being of service to others. Service is a divine expression and ensures ample receiving. Find what you prize the most in life - compassion, well being, money, laughter, sharing, working, animals, etc. - and allow the spirit of service to guide you. Service eliminates suffering, augments love and binds us together in light. Give thanks to the past - it will free your present. The past was not good or bad. It just was what it was. Nothing exists unless it is now. Now is the moment. Now we forgive. Now we breathe. Now we allow love to flow. Now we find our calling for service. We can step out of survival mode by joining something greater than ourselves (a group, an activity, a cause). Now is our life. Now is a miraculous instant where all is forgiven so that we can move on.

During over 20 years as a healer, I noticed that with many people there is an almost natural inclination to resist change regardless of how beneficial it may be for them. This fear is a choice to stay with the familiar and often oh-not-so-comfortable. Still, if we were stranded on a desolate island with little water left we would probably still hesitate to launch onto the sea to seek other, maybe better islands. We may think of the sharks in the sea, the crashing waves, but the reality is that by getting out of our comfort zone we act on courage and have a chance to improve our situation. When we take a courageous leap into the unknown, we seem to be in the presence of an angel in some shape or form that shows up to assist us. Courage is always action oriented. Courage is not the lack of fear alone, but the action present in spite of our fear. Acting through fear is not courage per say, for when we act from our fear we tend to be reactive. Courage is action in spite of fear - not out of fear. When fearful, acknowledge your fear, then list the benefits possible to attain in the end of the process. Now you can make a conscious choice to act in spite of fear. What is the worst that can happen? What is the best that can happen?

Our fear resides in our pain body. The pain body is the sum

of all our painful experiences, from this life and all others. When we're stressed out and fearful, our painful emotions and flashbacks collide with the present moment, draining our energy and pushing us to act in repetitive patterns of self sabotage, paralysis and ego-based behavior. Our soul incarnated here to this life in order to grow. Our pain body guards us to keep us in line with the lessons we need to go through in this lifetime. But our pain body can also prevent us from breaking through the same patterns. The pain body is our ego - the best ally and teacher which we have chosen to remind us of what really matters to us. The Universe is a mirror - all our feeling and thoughts are projected back to us. Our ability to manifest anything we want depends on this dialogue with the Universe.

The More You Love the More Love Finds You

Chapter Fifteen:
Rely Upon Miracles

The Dynamics of Miracles

We need miracles because we live within the boundaries of time and space. Time and space relate to the unchangeable reality, the span between birth and death. A miracle is a reaching out of linear reality beyond time / space paradigm to the realm of divine interconnectedness. When we invoke a miracle, we curve time and space and invite infinite healing to come through. With a miracle, all events past, present and future conjure and heal. With a miracle, all misunderstanding, fear based agreements and grief are healed. A miracle is like a rainbow shining through a dark cloudy sky. A miracle defies the laws of physics and gravity. It can be small or big. It affirms that there is more to reality than meets the eye.

We might explain away a miracle with technical rational, yet its timing defies all technical explanation.

Indeed, many miracles can be explained away, yet the very timing of their occurrence makes them unexplainable in ordinary terms. This is the nature of miracles.

When I was a student of *A Course In Miracles*, something very special happened. One evening we were learning about the reversal of time and space - namely accepting the notion that there is more to life beyond the way we see it. We used to meet once a week in my living room with a special older lady who was the teacher. One evening when everyone left, I went into the kitchen to have a glass of water. I glanced over at the coffeemaker which had a dial clock on it. To my utter surprise, the second-hand was going backwards! I looked again about five minutes later and I was sure that the minute-hand was also going backwards! The whole clock was going backwards! While it may have been true that this was an older clock, this had never happened before. Then, I got it! That evening we had just learned about the reversal of time and space and the clock which is the ultimate symbol of life, was going backwards! I checked all the other clocks in the house and none of them were acting strangely. I got my miracle. Time is reversible!

Time also represents aging. Reversing the aging process is a secret everyone seeks. But true reversal is not just about getting rid of wrinkles. Reversal occurs when we put the ego aside and allow the higher powers to come in. It's about surrender. By doing this, we connect with eternity and miracles occur. Eternity corresponds to the infinite and is the opposite of gravity. Once again we see that gravity is the force that draws us down to identify with time and space, ego and suffering. Eternity and infinity also correspond to the Universe. If we keep traveling through the cosmos, millions of light years, we end up reaching a place, an edge, there is nothingness. It is where time and space just stop. We don't really know what it means to go beyond it. We can only guess that there is more to time and space than we know. The vibration frequency of eternity is happiness because the Universe is in constant expansion. When we connect with this expansive mode we defy gravity and our vibration becomes one of increasing joy.

Attracting Abundance

Our income does not have to come from work only. When we manifest miracles, there are endless ways to connecting with abundance. We want to be current with the flow of life. Think of the word currency. Money has a flow. Abundance has to do with how we think. When we recognize abundance as infinite force, we'll attract more of it. Our ego, our fear and pain body are the stumbling blocks that resist abundance. It's hard to attract much love and abundance when we send fearful vibrations to the world. The Universe is a good listener and our job is to understand that there is abundance for us and we don't need to sweat the details. Our role is to ask, to believe we are receiving and feel the emotional joy now. Leave the details to the Universe!

Many people have the goal to get out of debt. Whatever we think about intently - we keep attracting. As long as we think about the debt we will keep endorsing it. Connect with abundance and it will gradually replace the mindset of lack. Visualize abundance geared up with joy and contentment. Feel how the Universe provides expansively, just like it has been doing since the Big Bang. Reflect on your passion and apply yourself to it. You must have something special about you – a special ability that cannot be taken away from you. Use this special gift freely and the Universe will respond with the miracle of abundance!

It is wise to take joy in other people's fortune. See any good fortune as proof that the Universe can provide generously. The second Chakra, also named the naval Chakra, is responsible for our creativity, money matters and sexuality. Things like trust, comfort and connection can all be connected to the second Chakra which falls right on the Water or emotional element. This is a reminder that our relationship to money is an emotional one. Any blockage in this area could hamper our manifestation in the world. Guilt and shame are especially notorious for blocking this area. Remove guilt and shame and you will allow the flow of creativity and manifestation into your life.

Ultimately creativity is the ability to create a lot from a little – something out of nothing. Living life creatively is about bringing our god-like attributes to our daily life. Our abdomen represents our second Chakra, the seat of creativity, sexuality and money. The second Chakra has a connection with the fifth Chakra (also called the Throat Chakra – center of expression) in that the fifth Chakra allows for its expression. So living creatively— creating our own miracles—means to live with a flow between the second and fifth Chakras: it is the connection between our center of creativity, sexuality and money and the center of expression that allows them to manifest.

With meditation and affirmation, we can gradually align our body and mind. Sometimes, as a result of severe trauma or misunderstanding, we have "Chakra displacement." This means that an energy center is not open or flowing. This can often happen due to cultural conditioning or personal trauma. Breathing intentionally into that blocked center can help to reverse this displacement. The Chakras are energy centers that need to be open and flow with each other. A blockage in any one Chakra will affect the others.

Seeing the Light

In looking at friends, partners and mates we often ignore their energy fields. We ultimately need to choose to be with those close to us based on how we sense them which connects to their level of awareness and consciousness. We are all inherently full of light, but it's our mission to recover it beyond layers of ego density. We can be acting on a low frequency (ego) in our daily life and therefore our light would still be hidden. Sometimes as children we were exposed to parents with lower frequency. They had to overcome many challenges and it was not always possible for them to provide us with safety. Consequently we may feel safer with people of similar energy as it feels most familiar. When our frequency is lower, we tend to avoid people of higher vibration because they seem to be "too much." Such a response does not allow us to live abundantly and freely. Our comfort zone often lies within that which we are familiar with.

**Very few of us were raised
in an environment that had
fluid abundance and consciousness.**

Often we were raised with people that were limited in their ability to provide unconditional love. In this state it was hard for them to contain much light. Later as we grow up we may feel comfortable in such environment. We will tend to attract people of similar frequency in order to feel safe. Although we may want to hold a higher frequency, we may not attract those who embody that which we want to become. We need to choose friends by the way we truly feel around them. It's about tuning in. The more light people carry, the more comfortable it would be to be in their company. "Like minded people" refers to the mind and not necessarily to the energy body! It is therefore not enough to search for "like-minded people" as it is to seek out "light-minded" people. It is more important to relate to others as we sense the light and awareness that surround them than to base the connection on mental things alone. This is how you heal along your spiritual path.

In our modern times, the notion that there is "no change" is obsolete. Change occurs all the time. Being stuck in the past hinders our capacity to change. By embracing change and putting our intention on the elements that feed us we move forward on the path of healing. What feeds you? What poisons you? Sometimes we can have a great day, just to receive that dreadful phone call from a relative who "totally sucks the energy out of us." But we can only be drained if we agree to it. When we match our frequency level with the draining person's frequency level, we allow them to engage in a harmful energetic exchange. However, when we do this between higher frequencies, this exchange is inspiring and nurturing.

Be conscious of the light emanating from people. This is not about judging others, but rather about developing our own observational skills. Feel them when being around them or even when thinking of them. Healing is faster when we create a reality that supports us and uplifts us. The more light we invite, the more we can share it with others. The more we recognize light in others, the more we carry it in us. The more light that we share, the more light we can attract from the Universe. Light is the essence of life and, like love, it is expansive and all encompassing.

Start by working on loving yourself and you already carry more light to guide you in your choice of friends, mates and teachers. The teacher always appears when the student is ready. There is an old saying: "When life gives you lemons, make lemonade." Identifying the "lemons" in our daily experience is easy. Every time a defeating thought comes up, such as a painful memory or a burst of anger - focus on this "lemon" and feel the energetic charge behind it. See how the "lemon" is a projection of your fear-body. Now add a new loving thought. As we already saw, love and sugar bear resemblance. It is not hard to see how by adding sugar (our own light sweetness) to our lemons (our painful life experiences) we can make lemonade (a delightfully refreshing life). This is the process of bringing light and creating miracles in our life. Enlightenment develops through attention and consciousness. It is the conversion of the density of our fear / pain-body into the lightness of our love / joy self! Every experience is "light" in disguise.

We tend to inherit behavioral patterns from our ancestors. These are generational patterns that are survival oriented and often ill adjusted to the ever changing life we live. When we heal our fear-body, the healing which is beyond time and space as behavior and feelings are nothing but vibration archetypes. When we change the vibration of our fear body the frequency affects all frequencies around us - to include our ancestry as present in our DNA. The moment of change is now - by recognizing the fear body in real time, observing it while monitoring our steady breathing and developing a sense of compassion towards ourselves. Compassion and forgiveness represent the interconnectedness of everything.

Everything changes in the Universe every second. No second is identical to another. Use this changeability as an advantage. It is a proof that nothing has to stay as it is - we are all in a constant motion of expansion. Ultimately, our pain and suffering dissipates as we identify more and more with our higher self and less with the physical body. This is the essence of enlightenment and a happy life. Overall, each experience we have can only occur within the parameters of our perceptions - our ego consciousness. Life sends us infinite signals telling us that there are more realities beyond the physical one. Most commonly what we call coincidence and "unexplained miracles" are a sign that time and space have more dimension than we perceive.

Believe & Receive

I was once presenting a workshop on the 4 elements. At some point we discussed how flying creatures can be a connection to the Air element and to the deceased or spirit-world. We went on discussing the subject when all of a sudden one of the students asked me if I placed a plastic eye on her water bottle. I didn't

155

understand what she meant so I looked at it and surely enough there was a small plastic eye, the type used in arts and crafts, glued to it! For a moment we all presumed that one of us was playing a prank, but no one was. We have no clue how the plastic eye ended up on the bottle. I remembered that in the beginning of the session I offered this student a glass of water. She said that she had her own bottle and lifted it to show me. I remember looking at it and it looked just normal. There was *nothing* on it. We never figured out how the eye got there. It was an amazing "miracle" with a possible message.

We noticed that this eye appeared after discussing the Air element and the flying creatures. Eyes are connected to the Air element (Head). The eye was on a water bottle and we know that the Water element represents emotion. Was this a message that the eye represented vision into the emotional realm? We looked at each other in amazement. How on earth did a plastic eye glue itself to the water bottle? Even if there *was* a rational explanation, it is the time and space that makes it a miracle. What matters is the end result *an eye on the water bottle.* You see, most miracles could be technically explained, but it does not take away from their miracle quality of manifesting in a specific time and space.

What we dwell on grows as we shift our attention to the ethereal dimension of reality. It becomes a natural part of our existing, an important station in the shift from identifying with ego to connecting with our higher self. Our higher self is the bridge to infinite consciousness which is the ever growing expansiveness of love. We have the ability to respond and be responsible. We are response-able! We can connect with the beginning and end of everything. This is the consciousness of infinity, the ongoing dialogue between energy and matter. It is the connection with the primordial knowledge - the knowledge that everything is energy - a flower, a bird, a thought, a feeling - it all exists in perfect interconnectedness and harmony. Most of our thoughts are generated in the Universe and not in our mind. Our mind is simply

156

amplifying universal frequencies that we call thoughts.

Thinking is all about tuning in.

We are here to be reminded of this connection between energy and matter so that we can dissolve our ego identification which only feeds our fear and pain. The journey is not one dimensional or linear. We manifest many opportunities to awaken and grow, as we radiate in a new light. As this takes place, more people are attracted to our presence, and more favorable events are unfolding for us. The Universe keeps sending its messages of serendipity and interconnectedness. When this happens we look more and more inside for answers as we are realizing that our connection with the Universe lives inside us.

The Power of Authenticity

To truly live our genuine life, to live our miracles, our sense of self will need a shift from ego-identification to higher-self identification. As long as our ego consciousness rules our life we can't really relax. We can't feel lasting satisfaction. The ego is like a black hole in the Universe that devours matter and we can never satisfy it. Most commonly, we only identify with money, family, work, status or ancestry. As long as this identification continues, we can't reach lasting satisfaction. None of these identifications truly reflect us. It is only a part of the greater "us" which only exists in illusion. Our ego is but a bridge to the bigger picture where energy and matter are interconnected through infinity. Past this bridge lies a life of authenticity.

Our real power lies in the present. The present is the only gateway to eternity, for eternity is beyond time and space. In other words, through the present we can connect with the true nature of life which is the multi-dimensional realm that includes the fraction of reality that we call our life. It is the "is-ness" of everything and it frees us to tap into our real power independent from fear and suffering. It is a point of realizing the illusion of pain. Recognize that your soul (and your higher self) is eternal; our fear is an illusion that holds us back through false identifications that are rooted in time and space. Just like our soles represent the ultimate gravity point, so does our soul connect with the eternal us. In this dialogue lays our life - between the demands of the physical world and the infinity of our soul. Ultimately, we can defy the gravity of time and space and remind ourselves of the miraculous reality that lives beyond the ego-based existence.

Our ego will most likely resurface as it can recognize our quest for ease and it would step onto our path to self-realization and growth. Total ego conquering may be hard to do, but the higher the "percentage" of our ego that we surrender to the higher self, the more sense our life will make and the more joy will be present. Sometimes there is a sense of grief when we part from old patterns of pain and suffering. Soon thereafter, though, our realization that the present actually contains less pain will take over. Saying goodbye or letting go of our pain can be challenging. Yet, it certainly pays to become one with our higher self and Spirit. Why would we want a friend that constantly inflicts pain and suffering? Embrace the realization that there is a way to defy suffering and ego. It's a journey into our real self.

When our real self emerges, we are more authentic and powerful. We accept things without judgment and we are free to listen to our inner guidance. We can have it all in this world while being free from its gravity. When we relinquish attachment and ego identification this world is ours to explore. On our journey we will encounter many miracles and opportunities to share in our light as we draw more light-based people and circumstances to us. Light is "contagious" and real. We are a vehicle for channeling the light as we dissolve our pain body. Gradually, as we look within, we'll feel a part of the Universe with its poetic wonder.

All is one. All is well.

Live a day without judging or labeling experiences as good or bad. You'll see how liberating it is to be in a space beyond judgment. To be in the moment is to release the past and renounce the perception of good or bad. Instead, label things as they are. You are what you are. She is what she is. It is what it is. This acceptance of others leads us to accept ourselves as well. As long as we resent something or someone, we keep our separation from it and therefore from ourselves. Ask yourself what the event and or the person was trying to teach you? As we thank the event or the person for the learning experience, our sense of self worth can become more solid. The Universe is not only a forest of symbols it is also a forest of mirrors where we receive projections of thoughts, beliefs, words and deeds. It's like standing in front of a mirror - who else can we see besides ourselves? Change your projections, change your image; the way you perceive yourself to be.

Into the Present & Out of Pain

As your actions are planted more and more in the present so will the real you come out and reveal itself. Nothing can threaten us more than our own fear and pain! Nothing can liberate us more than embracing our fear and pain as great teachers that come from love - the love of our higher self and the Universe! The female and male principles inherent in us are not just the people who created us - they are energies of universal balance. They represent reflection and action. To grow, we must reflect and act. Reflection is weak without action and action needs reflection to feed it.

Fear-based action is not true action. Only acts of courage are true - as they come from the higher self and can border on the miraculous. The Universe favors courage - courage is when we jump off the cliff knowing that it is only by jumping that the "angels" will hold us. This leap of faith in the very moment of being in between - is the reconciliation of the laws of time and space and allowing an intervention from another dimension to occur. Every act of courage, big or small, is a jump off the cliff to a new territory.

The reason our minds are so attached to what we know is that we carry a memory body that contains our experiences of this lifetime and others. It's called the body of pain, or pain body. Our ability to attract favorable circumstances and miracles advances our power and will. It's about moving out of our memory-body into the eternal and infinite knowledge of our soul. Our conscious minds are limited to what we absorb in any given lifetime. Only our soul has access to a dimension that defies time and space. As we change our thoughts, we change our circumstances. It does not happen overnight. It is a process. Be patient and allow for the shift to gradually happen.

Our body of pain, the ego self, acts like a transmitter. When we meet someone with a similar pain body we automatically connect. This connection is based on the lower resonance of the Chakras in conjunction with the state of the other person. We tend to be more familiar with whoever is like us, yet we are less likely to evolve through a mirrored energy block. The challenge and the miracle lay in connecting with the higher frequencies that heal us.

Like attracts like.

As you breathe gently, try to feel where in your body that you feel this "comfortable" feeling. Allow this area to relax. Next, ask yourself what this area wants to tell you? As you breathe, breathe into this area in order for it to relax. If this area is persistently sensitive it is a sign that this is one of your "pain body" centers. Interestingly enough, one of the most common pain spots is the chest. Many of us don't breathe in full capacity because of unresolved grief issues. We are unaware of the limitations of the lungs. If the ideal lung breathing capacity was placed at number 10, nothing would happen to us if it were at 8. But in the mind-body connection, a breathing limitation is the most common sign of unresolved grief.

Affirm: I breathe freely and with flow.
I open up my breathing
and release my need
to hold on to
conscious and unconscious pain.

When our conscious breathing allows us to feel body-less and pain-less, we can experience being in-the-moment, the true essence of time. Next time your pain body is triggered by things such as an argument or someone's negative remark - monitor how your responses and feelings are contingent upon your breathing freely and your ability to keep an ongoing connection to yourself. It is only when we limit our breathing that our pain body awakens. Nobody can take our breath away. To do so means to give away power and invoke old patterns of pain. Moments of pain and self doubt will always tend to resurface, but the ability to breathe freely while being in the moment will ease the pain and allow for fear to dissipate.

Remember - these are the misconception of ego: The Fear-Mind-Time-Space reality that keeps feeding our body of pain. Through our ongoing attention to the nothingness, we can develop an understanding of the illusionary nature of the ego. In the space of nothingness we can feel eternal love, one that is unconditional and forgiving, accepting and reassuring. It is in the very essence of unconditional love to ourselves that we can heal grieving, wounding and loss. Ultimately, by our mere presence, we can inspire others to be in that place, as true love is a power that defies time and space by connecting us all to the energy that lies behind our physical reality.

The ego's modus operandi is self preservation at any expense as it ties to natural survival instincts. The ego perceives many interactions as attacks and therefore responds in defense. Although the ego's patterns can be traced to survival, its automatic response would perceive many benign interactions as an attack on our existence. This automatic response maintains the status quo of the ego and the fear body. This zone in our self perception is very dense. When it is awakened, it shakes us to the core and acts as a drain. Our breathing becomes shallow and our pain body is set loose. Ultimately, we'll attempt to inflict the same perceived "hurt" on the other person. At this level, we act from a false identity and our soul essence remains hidden. By being reactive, we maintain the ego's reign.

By not responding adversely and by just observing, we can develop a sense of the real dimension of the event. Often other people are engaged in their own drama, their own need for self validation and love. They try to invoke our fear-pain body as a faulty attempt to seek validation. By not responding adversely we allow ourselves to remain conscious of our own soul identity. This response is effective as it contains a nucleus of healing.

The ego thrives on pain and drama.

Drama is often an attempt to ease pain. Since looking inside can be so painful we attempt to project our pain outwards as if it is not our own. By that, we turn the other into our "enemy" and therefore, the one responsible for our pain; it's all a game of mirroring. We grow by not acting from an automatic push-button mechanism. In a social conversation, we can often observe ourselves making a certain statement each time a particular subject comes up. Observe yourself as you say something else, or even not saying anything at all. Feel the ability to be yourself without

162

needing to contradict, please, assert or impress.

The art of not responding adversely is merely the ability to be in a space free from ego identification. It does not mean we should avoid expression. Rather, we are encouraged to be expressive and at the same time be aware of the choice not to respond at all, without losing our sense of identity. In fact, the more we are aware of the "nothingness" and "is-ness," we will be less judging and more accepting of ourselves and others. Our own density would dissipate and our identification will gradually merge with the higher self which is our soul connection. As the higher self defies the ego's identification with time and space, we merge with a dimension which is the real dimension; eternity.

Since the ego equals the mind, in that they are both linear, becoming aware of a reality beyond linear time can lead to less identification with the mind. Our thinking is not all of who we are. Our thinking will lead to expansion, but often within the realm of intellect and ego. To grow in consciousness means to be mindful of both thinking and awareness. Thinking is linear and ties to our self identification. Awareness does not need words, titles or attachments. It is free from the past or the future. It promotes higher thinking in that it helps to break through the boundaries of the linear self. In this space, intuition and guidance are strong, since our higher self draws on infinite knowledge.

This concept of ego versus higher self has to be experienced. True soul growth is the purpose of being here. All the rest may be mere facades of the ego. Soul growth is only possible by identifying ego patterns and promoting awareness versus being caught up in perceptions. This acceptance of non-attachment, and the release from the ego's confinement, frees us to live a fuller life that seeks a connection between all things. It allows us to live our life from a higher angle. Our participation in the laws of cause and effect becomes broader. Our life becomes rich with wonder and coincidence. The term Universe, one verse—one version—one united resonance makes sense now.

Acceptance can lead to change.

The Lessons of Pain

True healing is possible as we defy the grasp of the past and worries of the future. Entering the realm of timelessness invites forgiveness, love and soul realization. Often, the true way to "change" someone is to accept them as they are. When we do, we simply change our perception of them. With acceptance, the common denominators that bind us will prevail. With acceptance we forgive and let go of the hurt that defines our fear and pain body. Nothing real can threaten us for real things can only be love based. Love cannot threaten us, Love only heals. The main way to feel pain is through the mind. The body only conveys the relevant experiences as a medium. The body serves as a mirror from which we perceive our pain. Most pain we carry is mind-body based.

I often talk to people who have had an accident. My first questions are: "Which of your body parts were hurt in the accident?" and "What was going on in your life around the time of the accident?" Not surprisingly, many people report that before the accident happened, they had been through some conflict, chaos or confusing mindset. The areas that get injured are often a clue to what work we may need to do to better ourselves.

Healing can start with hurting.

In the metaphysical mind-body paradigm, our consciousness connects to our body and vice versa. So when a body part is injured, the body instantly sends endorphins and other chemicals to the area along with a rush of blood circulation. Sometimes a contraction occurs in that area in an automatic attempt to protect it from further harm. This mechanism of

164

contracting in response to pain is called "The Pain Cycle." The Pain Cycle's weak point is that when the initial contraction occurs after the injury, less blood circulation can arrive to the area as well as less nutrients and lymphatic flow. So, sometimes there is a short rush of circulation, but then the contraction takes over and halts the arrival of essential nutrients from the blood. This reduction in circulation causes the area to be less vital which then triggers an automatic contraction again in a faulty attempt to protect itself further. Luckily, this process doesn't go on indefinitely, because then the tissue would simply die from a total lack of circulation.

The Pain Cycle often stops somewhere around the point of causing us a chronic pain or a blockage. Many of us carry these weak points in our bodies and when we make a seemingly small movement in the wrong direction we injure it. We often see this point in the shoulders and the upper back. The back is a fascinating area, as the spine corresponds to awareness and the upper back corresponds to being emotionally supported and nurtured. The lower back corresponds to the material world and its support.

It is my belief that accidents are not just accidents. If a point of awareness and manifestation in the body becomes weaker- as in the lower back, which represents our flow of money consciousness, we can manifest an injury while lifting something heavy, stretching in a yoga class or simply sleeping on a poor mattress. The idea is that a weak point may manifest in various circumstances - all of which will end up at the same weak point in the body. The pain area always calls for healing. In fact, an injury is an attempt to attract attention to a specific area and is the beginning of a healing process for both the mind and the body.

**Everything that happens in the body
presents us with a healing experience.**

Physical pain is always preceded by an energetic counterpart, a concept, an emotion, an archetype, a conflict. The

165

more aware we are of our unconscious desires, and the more we allow them to be expressed in our daily life, the more vibrant our life will become. If, on the other hand, we have very firm ideas about how life should be lived, then it is almost impossible to be aware and acknowledge these desires, as they threaten the way we see life. Our instinct would be to ignore and/or block these desires from becoming conscious. At that very moment, we may manifest a symptom. A symptom is often a blocked energetic flow.

The more we are willing to challenge our resistance in acknowledging our desires, the more curable our symptoms will be. Conditions become "incurable" when we resolve to block the channels that link us to our subconscious mind. Just because something is not conscious does not mean it does not exist. Pain serves as a bridge to our subconscious, an attempt to show us a lack of energy flow or a blocked impulse. A symptom is a manifestation of a principle that is blocked or missing in our consciousness. We can safely say that our unconscious is our "shadow" - the part we don't see (and often don't want to see). Our self conscious is always attempting to balance our conscious level. Whatever we do not manifest consciously will always strive to show itself unconsciously. When we lose access to our subconscious, symptoms occur as an extension of what cannot manifest or is not allowed to manifest on the conscious level.

Symptoms are always a call for more awareness.
Pain is often a result of unresolved conflict.
Conflict, like guilt, always seeks punishment.

The function of the area where we suffer from the symptom can give a great deal of information about the message we are being asked to receive. For example, the abdomen has to do with digesting, accepting and integrating. The spine is all about support and awareness. The legs take us along our path. Through our physical symptoms we can find the messages that our

166

consciousness is trying to convey! Through healing we are forced to remain honest and within the oneness of mind-body, consciousness / sub-consciousness. It is always a journey to oneness. It is through symptoms that we seek to perfect ourselves. If you are seeking to understand a message that your body is sending you, reflect on the areas, organs or systems that cause pain and see what it could be conveying to you. You can read more about symptoms, their possible causes and the affirmations that may help in their healing in Louise Hay's books *You Can Heal Your Life* and/or *You Can Heal Your Body.*

Affirm:
Everything is perfect in my world.
I flow with love, acceptance and courage.
I am safe now.

Many of our symptoms revert back to where we denied love and chose fear. Therefore symptoms are illusion based in that the mind is fear-based and cannot truly exist in the love based reality. Through pain, suffering and "symptom-ology" (the art of reading into the deeper meaning of symptoms) we are reminded of where we swayed away from the oneness and love and, instead, gave the power to our fear based perception to dominate us. All fear is based on misunderstanding of the loving nature of the Universe. Love is the ultimate healing power. When our symptoms are embraced and become channels for self awareness they may disappear.

Although polarity is the nature of all phenomena, it is in the oneness that we find completion and peace. By observing all that happens to us without fear, we develop the essential bridge between conscious and unconscious. We can never become complete by just living peacefully. Conflict is unavoidable. Everything we repress will ultimately seek to manifest itself, often as physical or mental symptoms. It takes courage to address our shadow and subconscious parts and to reconcile them into oneness with our consciousness. The best tool to access this courage is through the power of love: Love yields acceptance, faith and knowingness. So, love all the chambers in your castle - accept the shadow, the fear, the resentment. Acceptance yields shift.

What you love becomes emancipated.

Behind many of our ailments lays repressed energy. Behind every symptom there is a purpose, a content that aspires to manifest. Many ailments are expressions of hidden, unexpressed conflicts. To access the source of these unresolved conflicts, one technique is to do free writing. For four to eight weeks write daily two or three pages of whatever comes to your mind. This exercise is intended to approach and remove our inner censor, that powerful voice that tells us "you cannot do this or you don't deserve that." Our innermost limiting beliefs, perceptions and conflicts may be expressed this way. If you wish to find more about this and other methods to tap into your creative self, see Julia Cameron's book *The Artist's Way*.

Holistically speaking, every condition we experience is contingent upon our willingness to manifest it. For example, a virus or bacteria can only cause an infection if there is some readiness in the body. It is often not just the mere exposure to them that causes infection as much as the body's willingness to allow them in or allow them to thrive once they are in. Of course, there are exceptions, yet we cannot ignore the possibility of a subconscious aspect that affects immunity and well being. Normally our bodies should have good resistance to disease. Yet, often we are being attacked in our weakest points that are points of least resistance. These points are known in medical terms as Locus Minoris Resistentiae, Latin for Points of Less Resistance. In medical terms these are "congenital weaknesses." In modern medicine these congenitally weak points often deserve no further interpretation and are often treated as "random locations." The possible connection of these locations to the mind / soul / emotional body is rarely looked at by allopathic doctors. Symptoms are often stemming from unresolved conflicts, inner imbalance (e.g. of the male / female aspects), issues with boundaries, blocked and unexpressed emotions or grief. Our symptoms hold messages of outmost importance to get us to know ourselves better and live authentically to our fullest potential.

Chapter Sixteen:
We Are All One

See No Separation

An important part of self realization is rejoicing in others' attainment and accomplishment and thus drawing on and resonating with the infinite goodness of the Universe; it means that there is no separation between us and them. We're all connected to the same unified higher power. To tap into this aspect of no-separation, we can ask for guidance by following these three steps:

Step 1: Surrender and acknowledge your smallness in the vast context of the Universe. We are only a drop of water in the ocean of life.

Step 2: Now that you are humble, acknowledge your greatness and uniqueness. Nobody like you has ever existed and will ever exist again. See that great things are ahead of you.

Step 3: Ask the Universe for guidance and protection.

When we ask, the Universe responds. It is amazing how by simply asking we are receiving, perhaps not necessarily in the same exact form that we had in mind. Now pay attention to your inner voice and allow it to come from a place of love and compassion. It is said that Jesus once met a blind man who wished to be healed. Although it was obvious that this was his wish, Jesus still asked him specifically what his wish was. Being specific with the Universe is the key. The Universe likes when we tell it exactly what we want. It mirrors back to us the frequency we sent to it.

In Voltaire's book, *Candide*, the protagonist, Candide, faces some very trying events that put him in great stress and danger. As he is forced to leave his comfort zone, he meets others who are also experiencing trying times. Candide's ironic ability to accept the worst without judging exemplifies the philosophical understanding that life takes us through various stations, not necessarily in the order we had in mind. Candide's approach to the present is "all that happens is for the best." In this holistic view, the mere fact that something happens, means that it has a meaning, otherwise it would not happen. Our greatness lies in our ability to let go of resistance, like the saying "let go and let god."

The Universe has bodily heavens (planets and stars). According to Astrology they all possess a meaning, especially the planets. For example, the planet Mercury governs thinking. Since our actions are greatly affected by our thinking, one can say that Mercury represents our thoughts put into action. Every ninety days Mercury goes into a reversal mode called "Mercury Retrograde." In this position, for 21 days, things just tend to "go backwards." Misunderstandings, missed appointments, accidents, problems with electronics - all seem to be more rampant. This is one way to view this celestial event. There is another side to all this, though.

Instead of looking at Mercury's Retrograde as a negative event, we can appreciate the chances it grants us in getting us out of a rut. By challenging our daily routine and interaction, Mercury

Retrograde allows us, or forces us, to respect and to re-examine the way we do things. It is as if it imbues freshness and renewal. Mercury Retrograde simply tends to take us out of our comfort zone. It is a necessary step in moving forward. Our comfort zone may only feel comfortable, yet in reality it can delay and stifle.

People who acknowledge fear are often not afraid to love. Love and fear are connected indeed. One is real; the other is made to feel real. The word "real" does not entail smooth or painless. It just means to see beyond duality and into the oneness. When we choose to love, we choose to align with "real." At the same time, even when we choose love over fear, we have to take into consideration the possibility of pain. Both love and pain are considered to be irrational emotions. So they do have something in common! In this context, love is not just a feeling or an emotion. It is a greater reality, a universal truth. In reflexology, the area of love is the heart reflex in the ball of the foot, below the big toe. Many people have a line / crease right under there, on the border of the Fire and Water boundary. This is called the line of separation and represents the impact that a possible separation has left on us.

Separation is "inseparable" from love. Separations can be powerful teachers. Often separations are assigned with the job to help us develop non-attachment, open our hearts and accept change. A separation can be a chance to grow. Grieving is natural, but living in grief stifles our soul and manifests in the lungs / chest area – the Fire element in the feet. When we develop a more spiritual understanding, we better see the transiency of life and that nothing was ever ours in the first place. It's all on loan anyways. Therefore, how can we truly lose something that was never ours to own?. Every major change in our lives is a kind of separation. For example, retirement: separation from routine. Separation is another word for change. Embrace change - because stability is comprised of ongoing change. Being in the moment, breathing and accepting, all help us to flow and use the power of change beneficially.

Accepting What Is

The main conditions under which change occurs is when we accept reality as it is - without trying to make it prettier. Acceptance is the first step, since most "stuck" situations stem from rejection of what is really going on. Accept that there is a reality beyond the visible. The more we allow the unknown to come in, by lowering our resistance to change, the more signs the Universe will send our way telling us we are on the right track. Be open to the flow, for flow is love and love is the only force that feeds our soul. By accepting love, we allow the Universe to work its special magic of defying time and space and performing miracles in our life. If you find yourself being cynical and skeptical, ask yourself if you truly suffer deep inside. If you do, then why refuse to open up to a possibility that you can tap into an energetic flow that is all inclusive and loving? What are you afraid of? Suffering stifles joy. We have to strive to be joyful at any cost, even at the cost of being silly. The higher self likes to dwell in joy, not in sorrow! Joy can open the heart and put us in the moment. Love heals our misperceptions. Only love is expansive!

Now is the moment to give up the confinements of the ego and the perceptions that come with it. Remember, life is not linear. The bigger the loss / challenge / grief, the more light is potentially hidden within it. We are here to unfold light and reveal it from underneath layers of ego density. Ask yourself "Why am I here?" and "What lessons am I here to learn?" Most likely our ego / pain body will provide answers that have one thing in common. They all have the potential to reveal the light of our soul to us. One of the most powerful ways the Universe conveys messages to us is through the new people we meet and listening to what they have to say. Try to truly listen, while minimizing your input. "Catch yourself" being tempted to say the same things you've always said. Instead, simply listen and observe how the new information is allowed to go deeper inside you. People, places and circumstances all convey important messages for us. Always keep a part of you that is open and receptive to outside inspiration.

It is our duty to take charge of our lessons while allowing others to learn theirs. Often, unhappy people seek to identify their unhappiness in others, in an unconscious attempt to ease their own pain. They will seek to project this pain onto others by judging them, provoking them, attempting to trigger a reaction. Signs of unhappiness are: dwelling on the past, our ancestry, things our parents used to say - anything that reflects not being here and now, and not taking responsibility for this very moment.

Seeking to blame or entitle ourselves to a certain group of people often comes from a need to justify our unhappiness. Over identifying with a country, ethnic group, nationality or social class only reflects the individual's unconscious fear that perhaps he or she is not competent enough. This over-identification separates us from one another. Many times these segregating concepts are an echo that just returns to the speaker. Our identity extends beyond that of a group. Being a part of a group is very important, but it should not come at the expense of developing a stronger sense of identity. The more we maintain an individual sense of identity the less power we would give away to any group, including our family.

Generally speaking, our attachments contribute to the way we think and act. As long as we carry strong attachments to ideas, things and concepts, our responses will be defensive and ego based, hence judgmental. Notice that often people who tend to judge frequently don't seem to be very content in their own skin. If we are open and flowing, being around those who frequently judge can prove somewhat draining, for they constantly seek to invoke our fear or pain body, the part we all carry that contains our unresolved conflicts. Happier people seek other like-minds (light-minds) and frustrated minds seek their own company. Nothing threatens the ego more than the refusal to partake in its follies. Shifting from a limiting fear / pain based mind to a detached, yet present mind - takes practice. Compassion toward ourselves and others is very important; compassion seeks to see the interconnectedness of all phenomena and to identify how we all choose to incarnate together in this time and space. This is how you heal along your spiritual path.

Chapter Seventeen:
Nothing is Random

There are No Accidents and No Coincidences

There can be no accidents. Although time and space are relative concepts, our presence on planet Earth is in complete alignment with them. We choose our circumstances. Since the definition of holism has to do with the fact that energy and matter are eternally intertwined, and that everything is interconnected, one can assume that there is no place for anything random to exist. Random is a contradiction of holism and, since holism is all there is, random can only be an illusion. Everything is tied to cause and effect, therefore nothing can be truly random.

If everything is interconnected,
nothing can stand alone as "random" implies.

It is by tapping into this interconnectedness that we can find the wholeness of being beyond "good" and "bad" - a true realm where everything makes more sense. Here are some common phrases that represent our holism: "There are no accidents," "Everything happens for a reason", and "It's a blessing in disguise." In our daily life, so-called "coincidence" plays a magic role. As we pay attention and notice something, so it happens more. This is a vibration message from the Universe.

I would like to share a story that happened one night as I was writing this book. It was getting late and I decided to go to the beach before it got too dark. I took off at about 6:30pm, just about when it gets dark in Southern California in September. When I arrived at the beach I took a random route over the sand. Suddenly I noticed a dark object on the ground. I picked it up, it was a cell phone. As I was looking around I could not see the potential owner so I took the phone and searched for a clue for their identity. I pressed on the contacts list and under "A" I saw the name Ariel. So, I thought that it would be fun to call another Ariel to ask whether (s)he recognized the owner's number. Then, when I pulled up the number I noticed it was mine! To say the least, I was a little puzzled. After all, how often would you expect your own name and number to be on a random phone you just found? I assumed the phone belonged to one of my clients and after calling another contact on the phone she *was* indeed one of my clients. When I called her, she said she had just returned from the beach with her dogs. She, too, was very surprised that I had found her phone.

We arranged for me to bring the phone to her house. I had not seen her for a year and it turned out that she was now pregnant and living with a shaman who is the father of her child. They invited me in for a healing session with a crystal light machine she acquired from "John of God" - a famous healer that lives in the Brazilian jungle. That day my writing focused on the Chakra energy systems - and here I am a few hours later having a Chakra alignment by my client whose phone happened to be found by me on the beach! What a coincidence? I had not been to that specific beach in 6 months at the time, and once I did, I happened to stumble on an object in the sand that led me to a healing experience and this experience resembled what I had written about that morning - namely, the Chakra system. I saw it as a sign that I am on the right path and everything is all right.

We live in a world of interconnectedness and any attempts to distort the connection will yield disturbance. The connection between things is not always apparent and has to be learned. Take a look at your life, your manifested reality. Do you still have passion in your life? Do you have harmony? Are you content or frustrated? Have you opened up to the possibility that all limitations are self imposed? The linear mind does not acknowledge miracles, those divine interventions that defy time and space. Yet, we do live in a multi-dimensional world. Sometimes we get a glimpse into this multi-dimensionality through our dream life. There exists a wide array of universal symbolism. Animals, plants, words, numbers all serve as conduits of inter-dimensional interventions. As you think and believe, so will your life be. As you open yourself to the unknown, growth can occur. The Universe is an echo to whatever we send its way.

Pay attention to how the Universe sends you messages about your life. Have you ever thought of someone and they suddenly appeared in front of you or called your phone? When I was a child I often thought I saw someone I knew just to realize when I got closer that it wasn't that person. Later on that day I ended up seeing the person I originally thought of. This happened so often that I was wondering whether the "real" person sent a double my way! Today I think this has to do with the laws of attraction and the message that there is no such thing as coincidence.

I was visiting San Miguel de Allende, a magical place in central Mexico. While there, I stayed in a beautiful small hotel. I had befriended the owners who had a rebellious thirteen year old daughter. Upon meeting the daughter, she declared that she wanted to talk to me in private. We sat outside the hotel and conversed. She told me that ever since she was a small child she's felt a strong connection with the world of nature. For example, she said that as a child she would see a butterfly flying by and asked it to fly over and sit on her shoulder. According to her, many times what she asked for was exactly what happened. Her direct communication with the butterfly was free of any interference. It was direct and pure.

She noted that her childhood was full of wonder, but she wanted to discuss her biggest fear with me. She was concerned that as she became an adult the childhood world of magic would cease to exist. She asked me "What if all this connection with nature was just a fantasy?" I thanked her for her trust in me and reassured her that there is enough wonder in life for those who seek it no matter how old they are. I said that nature can never stop from working its magic. Wonder is always there in many shapes and forms. It's up to us to find and seek wonder.

Nature is empowering.

We are all connected to nature for our entire lives. The Native Americans have the world of animal medicine or Totems. Each animal symbolizes aspects of the human experience and its connection to nature. Whether the animal appears in our dreams, a card we pull out of an animal tarot deck or if we actually saw the animal - it came to us to draw our attention. A hummingbird once sat on the water fountain in my yard for about 15 minutes. I never saw a hummingbird sit stationary for so long. It looked worn out and tired. I wondered if it was trying to send a message to me to look at myself. As hummingbird represents Joy, I was wondering if perhaps I had forgotten to take time and connect with my joy. I felt such a sense of connection with this hummingbird. I thanked it for its presence. I hope it got recharged and energized.

180

Chapter Eighteen:
Reality is a Mirror

Relationships & Reflections

When we fight looking in the mirror, we avoid looking inside. Often, this is the case with relationships. We tend to attract partners that serve as good mirrors. Usually, when we get upset with someone, we are actually upset with the reflection of ourselves as projected from the other person. Relationships can only be successful when the other person is, in reality, close enough to the image we have of them. We never truly know the other person 100% - but hopefully, what we project on the other person is close enough to what that person is. Just like it may be impossible to know ourselves 100%, it is even harder to know another person that well. Good chemistry is when there is some level of friction to challenge our comfort zone and enable growth; yet at the same time good chemistry entails that there is enough attraction to handle that friction. Friction is not "negative" for only the fear based ego judges positive or negative. Only with friction are we forced to acknowledge our mirrored shadow and truly work on ourselves.

Of course, we are talking about a little friction as opposed to lots of friction, for if a relationship is imbued with more friction than attraction, it may not survive. Many relationships reach a stagnant point as one or both of the couple begin to live vicariously through the other - this is called codependence. Becoming codependent can be very convenient in avoiding our shadow self – in the sense that we don't have to focus on ourselves when we are trying to fix another. Codependent relationships don't allow for much growth because the partners tend to project a lot onto each other - without taking responsibility for the fact that they are mirroring themselves. Therefore, being codependent means not being a responsible partner and not growing as individuals.

Simply put, we choose our relationships with partners and friends so that we can contribute to our natural growth. Ultimately, our goal with or without a close other, is to release ourselves from the grip of the ego. We can't heal the ego, we can only learn to recognize it and detach from it. We cannot heal an illusion, but we can grow out of it. Striving to be open, accepting and forgiving can help us to detach from the ego. When we start to let go of the ego, the process resembles that of mourning. Detaching from the ego-body that has been a part of us for so long can be painful. Just like grieving affords us a chance to be in touch with our soul, so does letting go, or attempting to let go of the ego. It paves the road to a soul-realized life.

Every walk of life is sacred even if it is different from our own. We are called by Spirit to honor all choices we make and others are making. It has to do with the recognition of the meaning of life. Even in times of chaos, if we pray for enlightenment, serenity can be achieved. Always give thanks for the gifts you already have. Ask for help by saying, "I don't know what to do next." When the ego acknowledges that it doesn't know, it allows the higher self to intervene because the higher self encompasses all knowledge. In order to ask for help, be humble and let go of your fears; this is courage and a call for action. This is what it takes to move beyond the ego. Action without courage is like a sail boat without a sail, we can only move when courage blows in our sail. Otherwise we just float on the sea of life, prey to our inner fears.

When we feel full of anger, it is OK to say "I'm mad as hell and I'm not going to take it anymore!" - And then harness that anger in a creative way. Sometimes courage can feed on anger; it can give us the power and energy to move forward. When you feel helpless, confused or disoriented, see how you can use your courage-energy to ride on a wave of faith. When you find yourself begrudging others for the fruits of their labor, do some hard work and see how the Universe sends you messages in the form of wisdom.

It is only by looking inside that we can see outside.

When we cultivate a sincere dialogue with ourselves, we become our own boss and we owe no one an apology for our existence. Assert who you are without ego; respect from others will follow when we are self respectful. Recognize who uplifts you by giving them your energy in return—as opposed to those who seem to take your energy away without recycling it. You don't have to defend your right to exist! You owe no one an excuse. Only the ego needs to defend itself. Our best strategy is to look at everything with neutrality just like the master who said, "Is that so?" There is a story about a Zen master who was blamed for impregnating a teenage girl by his village people. They approached him with the baby saying that he was his father, therefore he had to take care of it. All he said was, "Is that so?" and he took the baby. One day the real father was discovered and the villagers came to apologize and take the baby away. To their apology the master responded, "Is that so?" and gave them the baby.

When we give up the need for self defense, we choose to assert ourselves in all our uniqueness and beauty. If others perceive our lack of self defense as a weakness, it is their own egos that keep them playing games and ignoring their right to live an authentic life. Step out of victim consciousness by knowing that you have the right to be. We owe no one an excuse for our feelings, or our experiences. If we feel attacked we can exercise our ability to become energetically invisible. Visualize your body as a part of the surroundings, in that moment. Breathe consciously. By becoming conscious of our environment we can learn to foresee how things unfold around us. We can learn to feel how certain events unfold and know what the next natural step would be.

Our choice to live a dull, listless life may be our own self deception - a result of a belief that we do not deserve to have a fuller life. Within this lifelessness lies the knowing that if we only remind ourselves what excites us, we can start living again. Why are you hiding? There is a time to be visible and a time to hide. When we master the ability to know just how visible we need to be and when, we can have a wide range of experiences. By becoming proactive we start feeling events just before they happen and respond accordingly. We are always able to produce enough space for abundance.

If we attempt to pour a gallon of water into our cup, we limit our abundance. In order to receive more, we need to expand our receptacle. Our receptacles are our hearts and our minds. In order to expand them we can start by giving. Giving is the ultimate receptacle expander. Giving a smile is a good example. Those who cannot give a smile to us, may need our smile the most. Giving a reassuring word of empathy is always welcomed. Random acts of kindness are uplifting. Really, any giving is generosity in action.

Sometimes we may feel drained by things or people from the past. I find that asking Archangel Michael to sever the ties to these events helps. When you feel drained, start by recognizing the place in your body where you may feel discomfort. For example,

184

the abdomen or the chest are common spots. Now visualize a chord from that part of your body to the associated event or person. Now ask Archangel Michael, the Archangel of courage, strength and protection to come and cut this cord. This technique helps to release unhealthy attachments that feed on you and drain you.

Watch out for "takers" who don't give back. Be generous and put yourself first on your generosity recipient list. Just as when the flight attendant tells you to put on your oxygen mask first before helping others - only when we give to ourselves continuously can we truly give to others. When you find yourself wasting energy on self pity and feeling like a victim, turn it around by doing something nice for someone else – this is a win-win way to be generous and compassionate with ourselves first, while helping others. As we grow in awareness we see that life is not linear. Life has many dimensions and endless possibilities.

Every encounter in life is an opportunity to accumulate wisdom. When things seem to be chaotic turn to your inner wisdom for guidance. As we learn to trust our gut feelings, we learn that frequencies master the Universe and our only job is to remain faithful to our highest and best - the rest will follow. Not every experience is easy and flowing. Sometimes we need to swim upstream with our inner conviction and knowledge. By remaining faithful to our own wisdom, we will gain our own respect and the respect of others.

Pain & Purpose

Remember the story about my evening walk on the beach where I stumbled upon my client's lost cell phone? Well, when I arrived at my friends' house to give her phone back, she had a beautiful wolf-dog who greeted me by the door. It turned out to be a true mix of a dog and a grey wolf. I think the wolf in him far exceeded the dog. He was a socialized wolf. He was very friendly to me, although she said that he was usually timid. I remembered that in the Native American tradition the wolf is considered a great teacher. The wolf's message is to share our knowledge by writing or teaching others so that they can better know who they are and how unique they are. I still think that this wolf-dog manifested the lost cell phone just so that he and I would meet. In fact, my client dropped the phone while trying to leash this dog. I will never forget this beautiful message from the Universe.

What we fear most may become our reality.

Many people focus on doomsday theories and predictions and when we think "what if this or that was to happen?" the Universe hears us and responds! The future is not in form yet and it is our very thoughts and projections that shape it. Also, the Universe has no sense of humor. What we say/think/feel may become reality. Fears are best taken as signals that we don't feel deserving, loved or worthy. When we cultivate the notion that never before in history has anyone like us existed, nor will ever exist again in the future, we allow ourselves to breathe and be present. We become free of agreements that have no validation. Our fears and "negative thoughts" have a low vibration - low enough to resonate with anything dense and stagnant. As heavy thoughts take over, our breathing becomes shallower and we become less and less present in the here-and-now.

Because ego is a defiant fear-based perception, it always mirrors an "opposite" of the real self. All perceptions mirror a deeper knowledge in that if we reverse the perceptions and allow light to come through, they will automatically reflect a love based self - a self that has no enemies and no need for self defense. Practice "catching yourself" thinking fear-based ego thoughts; then stop the thoughts and reverse them with positive affirmations. This reversal will apply to past, present and future events, but you only need to take care of the present for the rest will follow automatically. We must strive to shape our reality in a love-based world. Every tragedy, illness or disaster in our life has a fear-based side. Reversing those very fears, through love-based thinking and affirmations, heals the events and circumstances in our life. In the fast and changing world of today, it is easy to lose our focus on love.

Only by reminding ourselves that we are here on purpose, and by choice, can we make sense of it all.

The quest for purpose is not a black and white search. Like a kaleidoscope, purpose has many facets. Overall, our purpose is to belong to the Universe and live every day as if we want to leave this world a better place. As long as we are caught up in survival mode, we are likely to act from our fight or flight mechanism, which is always fear / ego based. Emerging from our survival mode by reaching out to the real world outside us will keep us centered and in touch with the flow of the Universe. Imagine that you have already attained your goals. Now, how do you feel being a part of the world as you would like it to be? Is your world picture inclusive of others or is it all about you? As an exercise in clarity, come up with a strictly "ego-centered" goal and then come up with a purely "higher self" goal. While, of course, you are free to pursue any goals, always remember your "higher self goal" - the one that is soul-based, eternal and free from the limits of time and space.

Pain is fear's way of crying for love.

When someone is attempting to involve your ego and pain body, recognize it as a cry for love. Our polarized world feeds on polarity because it needs it to exist. Without black there is no white, just like fear and love are presumed poles. Fear and love mirror each other. Again, fear is illusionary from the standpoint of true love-based reality, but it is made to feel real by the ego. Next time you feel that someone is trying to provoke and harass you, just see it for what it is. There is no good or bad in it. Neutralize your experiences and then you will be free to feel true joy.

Neutrality does not mean a lack of enthusiasm or zest for life, it simply means being in a space of receptivity and "ego-less-ness." Take a moment to think about someone who hurt you dearly and the situation around which you felt the hurt - then release the circumstances as "just is." Everything is "just is." Billions of particles shift and change every second in the world and there is no point in endorsing a cellular memory that duplicates fear and pain. Of course, it is valid to process events, hurts and trauma. It is even more valid to seek to release the charge that is attached to them.

In being still, reality unfolds.

Take time to shake off accumulated excess of dense energy. Shaking off our hands, washing our hands with cold water, keeping a candle burning, taking a salt bath - these are all forms of releasing excessive energy that accumulates and contaminates us. All energetic contamination stems from fear-based consciousness and the ultimate way to purify absorbed contamination is to continuously shake it off and reintroduce love to our thoughts and actions. Even the strongest density grief and loss respond to the vibration of love. Nothing is permanent and the world is ours to be used on loan. Everything is in motion and as we tune into the movement of things life seems to flow more easily. We are always at the right place, doing the right thing, at the right time. This is how you heal along your spiritual path.

Love Conquers All

There is an old Latin saying that says that the root of evil is desire - Radix Malorum Est Cupiditas. The bottomless well of desire that we keep digging on our quest for happiness can become the source of our unhappiness. The source of our suffering is often stemming from the need to receive for ourselves alone without sharing. When we feel desire, we strive to satisfy our urge for what we desire, yet after we attain the object of our desire, we immediately move on to the next thing. And on it goes with desire. The more we can cultivate a sense of "being" with what we've attained, the more we overcome the "doing" of our desirous urges. A balanced state of being always invites a more balanced state of doing, but an imbalanced state of doing, which is a ceaseless pursuit of things, often leads to a poor state of being.

The more we were validated as children, the less we need to seek fault and fear in others in order to validate ourselves. It is never too late to validate ourselves. Talk to your inner child the vulnerable kid who was frightened and hurt and reassure him/her that all is well now. In order to truly acknowledge and release fears, we have to love ourselves. Otherwise, we may just project our fears onto others. Fear can entrap us in a vicious cycle where only the reintroduction of love can break it. Be willing to accept your own strengths and good points. Remember that no one has the power to take away our strengths. When we find and focus on our strong points, we cultivate a sense of sense worth.

When love is present fears dissolve

Fear seeks to bind us to the illusion that we are separate. Love unites. The more we hold on to loving and knowing ourselves, our strong points, the more we respond to people, events and circumstances with love and knowledge. Our response is contingent on how much we know ourselves. Knowing ourselves is

189

ultimately identical to loving ourselves. As we continue to catch ourselves in real time succumbing to ego and negativity, we can gradually turn each moment into an awareness moment, an opportunity to inquire as to why we need fear and negativity in our lives.

Our ego only attacks that which it perceives as threatening. Almost any situation can reveal that something or someone threatens us because any stimulus that can actually grow and transcend the ego can be seen as a threat. It takes more energy to get angry and contract, than to actively grow from an experience. Yet, the ego always prefers to set patterns of operation in life. *A Course in Miracles* teaches us that the ego is continuously seeking to contract and never to expand our awareness. Remember this every time you feel fear and negativity. Watch how even your own breathing changes in this contractive state. The ego perceives anything beyond its confines as unsafe and threatening. It's like living in a house and never leaving the bathroom. After a while, any confinement may seem safe and comfortable.

When we refuse to give ourselves the time and space needed to grow and attract new thought patterns, we may attract negativity into our lives. The nature of our soul self is ever expansive. See fear and negativity as opportunities to consciously shift from contraction to expansion. Some people have shifted through their creativity. Many of us have been told that we cannot paint or we cannot sing. Giving voice to our creative self requires getting rid of the inner voice that keeps repeating the "I can't" mantra.

Being creative does not necessarily pertain to painting or singing. Thinking creatively is as important. Creative thinking is in our god-like nature. God is often referred to as the Creator! Our inner critic often stops us from daring to express ourselves. Note that the mind is related to the ego and sometimes our minds, through fear, create so many obstacles that we don't even dare to toy anything new. This fear may stop us from leaving room for

190

new experiences. Remember the analogy of life as a dresser full of drawers. We always want to leave one drawer empty so that we can attract new experiences.

Do not be afraid to acknowledge your fears and shortcomings and to adopt a new viewpoint. It is important to keep our stress level at bay, for constant stress may steer us away from much needed inspiration and the gift of being present. If the fear of not being good enough, or being less than perfect, torments you - remember that the cemeteries are full of people that were good enough and "oh so perfect!" As you reflect on your life experiences, realize that you no longer need the good / bad polarity to recognize what or who you are - acknowledge that "it's all good" and always has and will be.

When we eliminate the good / bad polarity we allow the higher self to claim its domain and put us in the only place we can ever truly be - the present. Since everything is interconnected indeed, our inner worth always manifests outside of us. Since there is no true separation between the inner and outer, we will begin to recognize more and more the circumstances of our "outer" life are in direct connection to our inner work and inner worth.

Just how much we are interconnected can be seen in the following story. One of my students showed up to class looking sick. At the end of the session, I squeezed on a pressure point on her hands called "large intestine" which is between the thumb and the index finger. It was very sensitive. That evening when she got home, her twelve-year-old son asked her to rub that exact point on his left hand. The left side of our bodies corresponds to the mother. As she worked on this point on his left hand, he started to release long deep belches that he never had before. After this he felt better. This left her puzzled as it all happened just after we worked on that same spot on her same hand - unbeknownst to her son! It probably had to do with the cellular and subconscious energy we all carry, especially with our own family members.

The healing of the ego pertains to a reversal of time and

space and developing a new notion of their meaning. We often fall prey to the linear mind, the rational part of us that cannot accept the irrationality of miracles that stem from reversing time and space. When we let go of the rational mind's guard, we allow miracles to come forth. Miracles are a redefinition of time and space. This redefinition is the pathway to healing and evolving.

The realm of the miraculous is the realm of innocence.

When intention is clear we can experience a change of consciousness. We have the right to experience the magic of life. Our intellect may help others accept us, but it will not heal our inner child. When we seek answers, our intellect takes over, as we allow. The great mystery of life is never in accord with intellect alone. When manifesting a miracle, we defy time, space and gravity all together. In defying gravity, we let the guards of the intellect retreat which allows us to then connect to our inner child. Our inner children are innocently open to multi-dimensional experiences. Through innocence, intention and faith we can invoke miraculous interventions that come from an unknown realm - that which is the link between the visible world and the unseen. If our intellect keeps insisting that miracles are not real, we hamper our ability to visualize and manifest. Often we use rational as a smoke screen to shield us from the seemingly inescapable harshness of reality. Since ego and rational are close allies, it is only through our ability to imagine and dwell in that place of metaphysical space that we can manifest the healing that our soul seeks.

By stirring up drama, the ego conceals the magical realm which lies beyond time and space. Drama is often a faulty effort to regain "stolen" or lost energy in an attempt to heal the inner child. As you allow the inner child to prevail, you dissolve the rigid boundaries of the ego and allow for the interconnectedness of energy and matter to take place. Reflect on your childhood and on what used to make you joyful. The silliness and playfulness of a

192

child is nectar for the soul. Just as the hummingbird's mission is to spread joy or else be destroyed, our soul gets entrapped when we keep it confined in the ego.

Let go of your guard.
Free your ego / fear / pain body.

From the present standpoint, past hurts are water under the bridge and they are as alive as we want them to be! In joy, our spirit can dwell and renew itself. Open up your heart center and notice that grief and sorrow are just a mirror aspect of your joy! When our heart opens up we can feel the full dimension of life with its wonder and sweetness. The more sweetness we project onto others, the sweeter our own life becomes. This is not some romantic projection; it is a factual truth that sees the heart as the center of existence. The heart thrives on harmony and sweetness. How can the mind alone feed such a powerful center?

It is never too late to bring joy into our lives, as the doors of time are at our footsteps right now. We can choose to be free from the experiences and impositions that stifle our joy and inflict pain. Let go of illusion, for the only known reality is your joy and love. In other words, everything that is not joy and love is a misunderstanding, misperception and ego-based. Most likely we won't convert our entire life experience in one second, but we can develop, step-by-step, the observer in us that catches linear mind-based criticism in real time, and allows for joy and wonder to shift it. Start by observing the details of your present situation. See what portion of it is rooted in fear and what parts are based in love. Be grateful for the gift of the life you are already living and embrace it all with love. Check out The Seven Laws of Self Mastery in Appendix XIV for more ideas.

By owning all our experiences now
we can be united in a love-based reality.

Be Here Now!

All our achievements are due to universal providence. Just think how many things could have gone wrong along the way. Accept that we are subject to divine providence regardless of the degree to which we are in touch with the world of Spirit. Be grateful for all you have, the good and not so good, for these are all different aspects of one truth; everything is interconnected and no separation is possible in the Universe. Only the ego judges reality as good or bad. In our new discovered reality we may no longer need this polarity to shape our life. As we begin living more and more in the present, cause and effect seem to be more connected to each other. The invisible curtain that veiled our reality is being removed to reveal the bright colors of life. When we are living in the moment, everything has a stronger presence.

When you ask for help, acknowledge Spirit when you receive it. When we let go of fear and doubt, no one can threaten us and we see our pain as the illusion that it is. In the here and now, illusion cannot exist. The only true time that exists in the Universe is the here and now. The here and now is free from pain and fear. Any remnants of our pain and fear can hamper our ability to be present. In the here and now, we have no enemies, our ancestral suffering is healed and our need to identify with pain is obsolete. In the here and now, we stop missing the notes in the loving song of the Universe because we are in tune with its frequency. As we gradually allow our density to dissolve, higher frequencies can flow through us. As we choose to participate in the flow and by becoming a part of it, we feel more fulfillment, wonder and joy.

**In the flow,
we have nothing to lose,
only to regain our well being**

Free yourself from mental preoccupations and expectations. If you are a perfectionist, cultivate self forgiveness. Often, truer reality lies in between everything we perceive as true reality. Work to reduce judgmental thinking, for there is a whole middle ground between good and bad. When we let go of judgments, we not only live in the present, we also embrace that which is not known yet, and thus allow for the miraculous to prevail. Allow for your own deep healing to take place, free of external interventions. Let go of limiting people, thoughts and perceptions. Truly accept that life has its flow and your job is to tune into it! Release any painful feelings of being alone, for you are becoming aware of a greater reality.

Exercise your ability to expand your experiences by stepping out of your comfort zone and having the courage to live that which has not yet been lived. It is your divine right to be just who you are. We are an instrument for enjoying life's gifts. Do not worry about the future. As we embrace the unknown, we allow for everything to happen at the right time and the right place. Trust in the process of life and the existence of a realm beyond the perception of the senses, this is the realm of the Universe, where all is one – indeed.

~Part III: Appendices~

Appendix I – The Four Elements Chart of the Feet & the Emotions

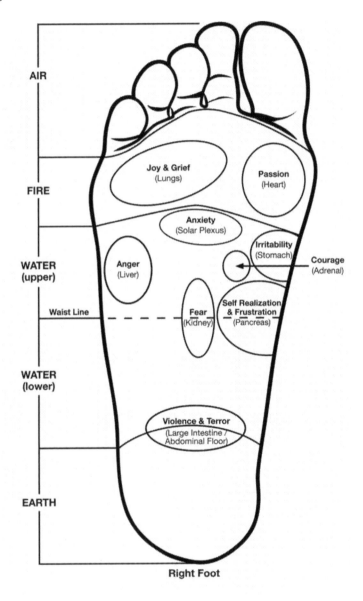

Right Foot

The Four Elements Chart of the Feet & the Emotions (cont.)

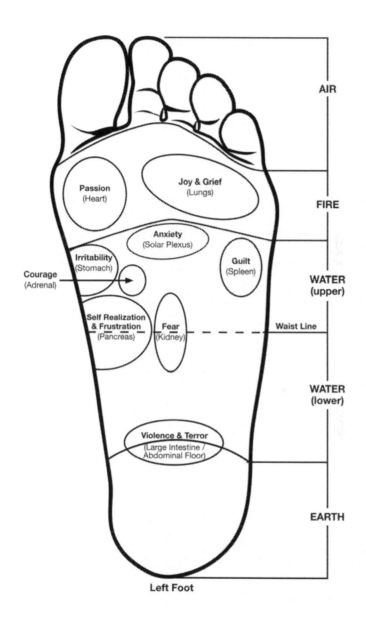

Left Foot

Appendix II – The Toe Reading Chart

Toes	1st Big Toe	2nd	3rd Middle	4th	5th Pinky
Emotion	Grief connects to the lungs, to the soul and to past incarnations.	Joy connects to the heart, to the core and to the here and now.	Fear connects to the kidneys, to the ego and to the past, present and future.	Anger connects to the liver, to the shadow and is a result of fear, therefore connecting past, present and future.	Passion connects to the gut, as well as the here and now.
Trait	Forgiveness, Letting go.	Inclusiveness	Discernment	Release	Wonder
Body Area	Head	Chest	Diaphragm	Abdomen	Pelvis
Organs	Lungs, colon	Heart, Circulation, Small Intestine	Kidneys, Bladder, Immunity	Stomach, Spleen, Pancreas, Liver	Uterus, Gut, Prostate, Genitalia
Energy Center	Thinking, Perception	Habits, Movement	Balance, Instincts	Emotional Center	Creativity, Sexuality
TCM (5 Elements)	Metal	Water	Fire	Earth	Wood

Western (4 Elements)	Air	Fire	Air / Fire & Water / Earth Boundary	Water	Earth
Odor	Rust	Burnt	Moldy	Sweet	Rotten
Result	Clarity	Rhythm	Balance	Well-being	Product-ivity

Appendix III - Elemental Imbalances Quiz

You can identify your core elemental imbalances through this quiz. Using a pencil, circle the answers that feel correct. Remember to go with your first instinct. Select what most feels like you. On a scale of 1 to 5—1 being disagree strongly and 5 agreeing strongly—mark down the appropriate answers.

Then read the following sections on the Analysis of the Elemental Imbalances Quiz Results. Once you understand your imbalances, take the appropriate action needed to rectify them with the Elemental Balancing Exercises which follows.

Elemental Imbalances Quiz Key

1 = Strongly Disagree
2 = Somewhat Disagree
3 = Somewhat Agree
4 = Agree
5 = Strongly Agree

Air

1. Between activities and when resting I often day dream.

○   ○   ○   ○   ○
1   2   3   4   5

2. I often have vivid dreams, rich in colors and symbols.

○   ○   ○   ○   ○
1   2   3   4   5

3. I often seek to expand my horizons through popular culture (e.g. movies, books).

○   ○   ○   ○   ○
1   2   3   4   5

4. When I think I often hear an inner voice of guidance.

○   ○   ○   ○   ○
1   2   3   4   5

5. I tend to over think as opposed to taking action.

○   ○   ○   ○   ○
1   2   3   4   5

Fire

1. I am passionate about my daily activities.

○	○	○	○	○
1	2	3	4	5

2. I easily take action when needed.

○	○	○	○	○
1	2	3	4	5

3. I am a creative person.

○	○	○	○	○
1	2	3	4	5

4. I love easily and freely.

○	○	○	○	○
1	2	3	4	5

5. I am a dynamic person who doesn't often procrastinate.

○	○	○	○	○
1	2	3	4	5

Water

1. I don't feel fear very often.

○	○	○	○	○
1	2	3	4	5

2. My digestive system works well.

○	○	○	○	○
1	2	3	4	5

3. I often reflect on the mysteries of life.

○	○	○	○	○
1	2	3	4	5

4. I easily tap into my intuition.

○	○	○	○	○
1	2	3	4	5

5. I can easily sense other people's feelings.

○	○	○	○	○
1	2	3	4	5

Earth

1. There is nothing wrong with my sexuality.

○	○	○	○	○
1	2	3	4	5

2. My instincts provide me with safety and security.

○	○	○	○	○
1	2	3	4	5

3. I don't often accumulate much clutter.

○	○	○	○	○
1	2	3	4	5

4. My childhood was safe, warm and joyful.

○	○	○	○	○
1	2	3	4	5

5. I don't feel that having a lot of money can fix everything.

○	○	○	○	○
1	2	3	4	5

Appendix IV - Scoring & Analysis of the Elemental Imbalances Quiz

Now, add up your scores for each individual element. Then compare each of the totals with this scale.

5-10 = Elemental Deficiency
11-20 = Needs More Work
21-25 = Fairly Balanced

This next section addresses each individual element and offers advice if you got a score under 21 points on any element. It addresses how to better incorporate the elemental flow into your life. Start with your lowest scoring element and work your way up. The lower the quiz score, the more necessary it is for you to read and apply the techniques and lessons for that element.

Air

The Air element corresponds to the Head: thinking, dreaming, meditation, wisdom. To improve Air energy flow, consider paying more attention to your dream patterns. If you don't remember your dreams, voice your intention to recall them upon waking. Seek out and attain a good dream interpretation book. This is also a great tool for intuition development. When you wake up, sit and write random thoughts with no respect to coherence or social convention. Do this every morning for up to two months during which you are not advised to read your writings. Try to accomplish three pages daily. This process helps to eliminate the inner critic that affects us all from an early age.

The Air element corresponds to the blue color in the sky. When outdoors, reflect on the breeze and gaze at the horizon. Meditation, prayer and affirmations also help us to tap into our inner wisdom and to free our thinking. When you feel stressed, observe your breathing patterns as this can indicate your ability to stay in the present. If you notice that your breathing has paused you could be stuck in the process; if it has quickened you may be rushing through the process. There is a connection between the brain and the intestines. Therefore, improving digestive function is very important as well.

Pay attention to serendipity and coincidence. Air represents the infinite and the channel to draw on our infinite source of inspiration and guidance. Think of yourself as a tree whose branches always strive to grow in their tips. Inherent to the human experience and self-realization is the ongoing process of growth. We never know everything and being open to ongoing learning of any kind is the key to maintaining our mental and spiritual faculties, the essence of the Air element. See the 22 Spiritual Laws and Inspirations in Appendix XV for more guidance.

Fire

The Fire element corresponds to the chest: lungs, heart, ribs and upper back. It also corresponds to the muscles. To improve Fire flow take a look at your aspirations, maybe it's time to really find them. Note the connection between the word aspiration and respiration. They all have the same core as the Latin word for spirit. Fire is the element that wants to expand, grow, achieve. It is the ego; I want, I do. It is an element that contains power and the ability for self expression, including personal charm. A major factor in developing the Fire element is cultivating courage. Becoming more courageous is the key to the Fire flow in our life.

These are some options to cultivate courage:
- Build your competence to stay present and act while afraid.
- Practice faith and patience – taking positive action for which you see no positive outcome, immediately or ever.
- Learn by experience through stories about others overcoming their fears.
- Create and embody a life story outside your comfort zone and beyond survival mode.

Courage is the ability to step out of time and--in that moment of eternity--acting or speaking in a way that embodies love, compassion and wisdom. Seek to become more dynamic by emphasizing action over thinking. Spiritually speaking, our goal in this lifetime is to shift from an ego / conditional love based life to higher self based / unconditional love. Practice unconditional giving and unconditional love by performing random acts of kindness. A good tool to improve dynamic action is monitoring our response to rhythm. While listening to music focus on the rhythm, feel it inside you. Move and dance; this will also activate the Fire element. Rhythm is identified with the heart Chakra, just like the heart beat. When you hear crickets remember your heart Chakra and its need to be in rhythm with the Universe. Identify your rhythm consciousness. When you walk, monitor your pace, see if it's rhythmical. You can find rhythm everywhere, inside and out. The more we connect with the rhythm the more dynamic action is capable of happening. All in all, the core of the Fire element is unconditional love which is possible through harmony; giving for the sake of giving. Ultimately, Fire is about doing and acting. I do therefore I am.

Water

The Water element connects to the abdominal: kidneys, intestines and part of the bladder. Water represents the body fluids: blood, urine, intestinal fluids, lymphatic fluids, bile, hormones and spinal fluid. Water is needed to purify an individual. The food we eat corresponds metaphysically to the ideas we digest. The better we accept and flow new ideas and concepts the better our digestive system will be. It is a changing element that corresponds to fear and other emotions.

To improve water flow, examine the dialogue that exists between you and your subconscious as the Water governs the subconscious. A key to connecting with the subconscious is connecting with dreaming. Like the Air element the Water has a connection to dreaming and the messages inherent in it. Most dreams from the Air element (processing our daily experiences) stem from our conscious mind. The Water based dreams are anchored in our subconscious mind and can be of higher importance though they are less common. The subconscious mind as represented in the Water element is somewhat ahead of us; it is often pre-monitory in that it reflects on events that are about to happen in the near future. Dreams can be also a combination of the elements thereof.

Water represents the uncontrolled flow in our life. Allowing our subconscious to express itself does not mean to lose control of our life, rather let go of the control (fear and ego based) and allow our subconscious intelligence take over.

One of the most common signs of water blockage is constipation. If you experience constipation (physical or mental) examine the following themes:

- Renewal – Do you allow space for the new? Imagine your

life as a dresser with fully loaded drawers. Emptying even one drawer will invite the new.

- Giving – Any giving of ourselves is giving to us. Give freely to others, just as you would like to give to yourself.
- Taking – You deserve to receive. Allow yourself to take. True giving is only possible when we know how to take.

Earth

Earth corresponds to the pelvis, legs and feet. The Earth element has the strongest gravity for it is the heaviest element. It corresponds to elimination of toxins and of material the body no longer needs. Other attributes of Earth are possessiveness, accumulation, beauty, sexuality (aside from maternal instinct) and slow and lengthy processes. Earth connects to the earthy life and its basic needs. Eating, drinking, sleeping and having sex.

To improve Earth flow in your life, examine your attachments and why they are important to you. Reflect on what you can let go of. Oftentimes we hold onto things that no longer serve us. Gardening is a great activity to improve Earth flow. Make sure you have live plants in each room of your home. People with a green thumb usually have a great grip on this element. Note the connection with the Water element in gardening and Earth cultivation. Your emotional flow (Water) feeds your basic needs (Earth). Together they produce growth.

Appendix V - Elemental Balancing Exercises

In your journal, date your entry and write your responses to the following exercise suggestions. First, select a time when you will not be disturbed and can devote your full attention. Then, put yourself in a quiet place with good lighting. Lastly, follow your intuition when doing the exercises, be thorough and avoid judging or censoring your responses.

Air Exercises

Air Exercise 1
Meditation is the greatest tool for balancing the Air element. Find a quite place and release tension from your body. Use visualization, affirmations and reflections while maintaining a natural breathing rhythm. Visualize positive outcomes and notice changes in your breathing patterns. It is important to align the breathing with your thoughts. Reflect on your meditations through writing.
Air Exercise 2
Improve communication. Write a letter to yourself. Express your feelings and thoughts. Be sincere and straight forward. Place the focus on being constructive. After internalizing what you've written, feel free to write a response with goals and ideas for change. Every once in a while keep this correspondence by writing a new letter.
Air Exercise 3
Media is powerful. Pick up 1-3 CD's, movies or art forms you don't usually fancy. Observe your thoughts and feelings as you are listening or observing these forms of media and write down what comes through in your mind as you expose yourself to

different perspectives of expression. The ability to better understand what we don't normally connect to can help to deepen our flexibility and adaptation skills.

Fire Exercises

Fire Exercise 1
Take a few minutes and think about having the opportunity to live life all over again. What would be the one thing you would be passionate about? Why? After you write about the nature of your passion, consider how you are incorporating it into your life now and what steps you can take to make it more present.
Fire Exercise 2
For the next week practice random acts of kindness whenever the opportunity presents itself. It can be as simple as holding a door open for an elderly woman at a restaurant, or asking a stranger how he or she is doing. Do not expect anything in return whatsoever. Write about how these acts affected you.
Fire Exercise 3
Take a walk while monitoring your breathing and your pace. Alternately, sit down and monitor your breathing as different thoughts cross your mind. It is important to let the breathing flow independent of the different thoughts. Afterward write down any reflections that came to mind regarding this activity.

Water Exercises

Water Exercise 1
Reflect on a fear that you have. What are you afraid of and why? If you could, what steps would you take to remedy this fear?
Water Exercise 2
In the next week before going to bed reflect on your feelings about the day to come and write what you would like to see happen. In the evening the next day, reflect on the correlation of what happened that day and what you foresaw taking place.
Water Exercise 3
Drink more water, even when you are not thirsty. This will present the body with more water flow and therefore nourish the Water element. If you feel differently write down the contrast.

Earth Exercises

Earth Exercise 1
Make a list of all your major attachments and note how they serve you. On a scale of 1-10 denote how important they are to your life, 10 being the most important. Consider which are no longer necessary and reflect on why they are still in your life?
Earth Exercise 2
Pay attention to the plants in your living environment, making sure they are well watered and fed. Remember that our plants are often our mirrors. If your plant isn't in the best condition, what could it mean to you? Keep a log of the possible changes you notice about the plant life surrounding you.
Earth Exercise 3
Dust and clutter are representatives of the Earth element, they represent stagnation. Reflect on your home and how it represents you. Get rid of clutter. Clean your fridge of expired food. Reflect on your objects and furniture, the colors, shapes and see how they possibly correspond to you. Remember in what mindset you were when you acquired them or how you felt the first time you saw them. If needed rearrange items in your space. Take the appropriate action necessary to clean your living environment and write for ten minutes about how you feel afterward. Be sure to reflect upon the possible parallel between your house being neater and your feelings.

Appendix VI - Numerology Chart

1	Initiative, Beginning, Originality, Strength, Leadership Number one is the original number and therefore stands for originality. It is the number of the pioneer, someone who made something from nothing. God is number one. One is the first encounter of creation and the beginning of a process. Remember your first kiss, the taste of a new dish, the first time you drove. One stands for the ability to respect, to see again and to see something as if it was the first time. A new sight, a new vision. One is the freshest of all numbers. Dynamic, visionary, demanding.
2	Duality, Harmony, Balance, Artistic, Reliable Two represents duality and the meaning of the female energy and the male energy. It is also the earth and the sun, the sun and the moon, light and darkness, Yin and Yang. The process of duality is omnipresent. We all have male and female within us. In healing, working through the polarity of two is essential. We work with too much versus too little. We try to move dense energy to places where it is less dense. In essence, two in balance becomes a one. The phrase "as above, so below" is a classical two (see also 6). When above and below merge, life is in its full force. Self-sufficient, tolerant, forgiving, shy.
3	Solution, Results, Understanding, Expressive, Self Centered Three represents the result. It is the meeting of one and one that become three (1+1=2 unless a new entity is born of the meeting: 1+1=3). When one and one becomes two you simply add the components. As one and one become three a new entity is created, like a baby. A new life. It is only by the result that we know what has happened. Three is the spiritual number and in many folklore tales miracles and wishes come in threes. Three is a charm. In a healing session, the healer brings his best and the client brings his best. The result is a new creation. In dream

	work three is a spiritual number and represents the presence of Spirit. Creative, talented, popular, charming, fickle and witty.
4	Security, Stability, Thoroughness, Foundation, Reliable, Loyal Four represents the planetary aspects. The Four Elements (Air, Fire, Water, Earth). The four seasons and the four directions. For example, to understand a person we can see him or her through the imbalance / balance of the Four Elements. Logical, builder, didactic and practical.
5	Learning, Wisdom, Changes, Passion, Adventure, Moods Five corresponds to the cosmic energies and The Five Elements: Metal, Fire, Water, Earth and Wood. The pentagram represents the human body. Fives are free-thinkers with a touch of flamboyance and drama. They experience many changes.
6	Humane, Vitality, Social, Peacemaker, Charm, Intelligence Two triangles. Twice three. As above, so below. Men versus the creator. In healing the number six connects to the practitioner as a channel for higher energies. He or she needs to fine tune constantly in order to remain receptive to the requested vibrations. Home lovers, meddling, caring.
7	Mystical, Intuitive, Calculating Seven energies compose the spectrum; there are seven layers around the Earth, seven notes in music, seven days and seven Chakras. When the 7-tone rainbow occurs it is an indication of a certain connection between creation and nature. 7 people are mental and pensive, can also be stand-offish.
8	Infinity, Power, Money, Success, Fortune Eight is the connection to the infinite as well as cycles. 8's may be successful, charitable, power hungry, courageous, ambitious, leaders, reliable and vain. Wise and trustworthy, they can also suffer from self-pity and depression. 8's stand out as fortunate and lucky in money matters.

9	Romantic, Intuitive, Leader, Intelligent, Universal, Completion Nine months represents a gestation period. Out of a persons' mind, a constant birth takes place. The result of the interaction of the two hemispheres. Nine is completion of a cycle. After nine we revert to ten and therefore one (10 is 1+0=1). Nine brings the notion of renewal, birth. Nine is a combination of four and five. Four and five are the combinations of the physical set and the spiritual. There is an ongoing meeting of matter and energy. Highly sensitive and responsive, 9's are leaders, emotional (sometimes over-emotional) with a touch of self pity and a romantic flair.

Appendix VII – Foot Observation Chart

The following chart is based on The Four Elements and ends with general mind-body observations of the feet. The big toe is toe number 1 and the pinky is toe number 5, with the other toes being number 2, 3 and 4 respectively. This chart can help you to understand the logic behind the observations. It is for observational purposes only and is not intended for diagnosis.

Air - The Toes - Head

Ingrown toenail	Chronic headaches or migraines.
Toe pads are swollen and red	Acute sinusitis.
Toe pads with hard skin	Chronic sinusitis.
Children with swollen pads	Hyperactivity.
Toe 5, the pinky, is bent, red and calloused and / or hiding under toe 4	An irregular menstrual cycle, difficult menopause in women and prostate problems in men.
Various marks on toe number 4 and 5 (such as creases)	Hearing problems, vertigo and hearing ringing in the ears. A beauty mark in the middle of toe number four is balance problems.
Hard skin on the dorsal part (top) of toe 1	A condition in the neck vertebra and pressure that can cause dizziness, vertigo and even fainting.
Hard and dry skin on the mid-lower part of toe 1	Pressure on the hands that can cause numbness, Charlie horses.
Deep crease on toe 1	Whiplash.

Redness in the planter base (bottom) of toe 1	Sensitivity in the throat, aptitude to losing voice and repetitive inflammations.
A crease in the planter base of toe 1	Could be tonsil surgery or tonsil problems.
Creases on the toes	Inflammation in the head.
Marks under the nail and discoloration or fungi under the nail	A problem with teeth, gums and hair.
Numbness in toes 4 and 5	A pressure or other problem on L4 and L5 of the vertebrae.
Numbness in toe 1	Pressure or other condition in C1 or C2 vertebrae.
Toe 3 is very short or very long (in relation to the neighboring toes)	An imbalance and immunity condition, a mental and emotional imbalance.
Bowed nails with dents or marks	Can reflect possible brain damage.

Fire - The Ball - Chest

Dry, hard skin under toe number five and rigidity in the joint	A condition in the shoulder joint.
Raised, inflexible toes with strung tendons on the dorsal part	Tension in the neck and shoulders.
The tone of the tendons that connect with the toes (whether too tight or too loose)	The condition of the upper back and chest.
A crease on the area under toe 1 and 2	Asthma.
The entire fire area: dry, hard, gray	Excessive smoking. Angina pectoris and emphysema.
A small dry area surrounded by redness, on middle dorsal side	Mastectomy.
A red area, very warm, full, swollen and sensitive to the touch, with pronounced redness under toe 1	A serious heart condition preempting a heart attack.
An old crease under toe 1	Past heart attack.
A very vertical crease under toe 1	Open heart surgery.

Water - The Arch - Abdomen

Deep creases in the middle upper arch	Stomach problems, ulcers.
Red creases	An active ulcer.
A star shape in the upper arch under toe 3	Diaphragm hernia or tension.
Horizontal marks in the upper arch under toe 3	Forced breathing.
A dark mark on the right foot under toe 4 in the upper arch	Gallstones.
Marks on both feet in the upper arch under toes 4 and 5	Liver and spleen area allergies.
Marks on both feet in the upper arch under toes 4 and 5, and an additional line on Fire area between toe 1 and 2	Allergic asthma.
Marks on both feet in the upper arch under toes 4 and 5, and an additional marks on the toe pads	Hay fever, an allergy that affects sinuses, eyes and ears.
Marks on both feet in the upper arch under toes 4 and 5, and an additional mark on the upper Water area under toe 3	Food allergies.
Marks on both feet in the upper arch under toes 4 and 5 and no additional marks on these areas	A skin allergy.
A long line-R foot under toe 4	Old jaundice, liver condition.

A deep crease on the left foot under toe 4	An old fever disease and tendency for fever.
A long deep crease starts in Fire under toe 4 goes all the way to the heal (R foot)	Arthritis or joint sensitivity. Sometimes poverty in childhood.
Red marks or small blisters under toe 1	Colitis.
Horizontal lines and dryness	Chronic constipation.
Vertical lines and moisture	Chronic diarrhea.
Inter-crossing vertical and horizontal lines	Tendency for diarrhea and constipation.
Dry, hard skin	Diabetes.
Dryness in the middle of the Water area, under toe 3	Kidney conditions.
Creases under toe 3	Not drinking enough water.

Earth - The Heel - Pelvis

The area under toe 1, on the heel, is swollen and red	Acute inflammation of the bladder.
The area under toe 1, on the heel, has hard and dry skin	A chronic bladder inflammation.
A line between Water and Earth areas	Cesarean, hysterectomy, abortions, difficult births.
A crease under toe 1	Lower back conditions.
A very dry and hard heel with red dots and sensitivity to touch	Sciatica.
Lump in the heel area	Chronic inflammation of the pelvic area.
Deep creases around the bottom of heal	Hemorrhoids.
A short thick and inflexible Achilles tendon	Shortening of the lower back muscle and tendency to menstrual pain.
The area around the ankle is swollen	Menstrual pains, pregnancy or circulation problems. Could also be related to kidney function, lymphatic and endocrine systems.
Difficult rotation of the ankle joint	Lack of flexibility in pelvis.

General Observations of the Feet

Full red warm foot	High blood pressure caused by stress.
Foot is pale, cold, soft, dry	Low blood pressure.
When you join both feet base-to-base and compare the arches	Scoliosis, if the arches are different.
Surgeries	Surgeries will often show in a straight crease in the area of the surgery.
Musculature	The state of the muscle in any area of the foot indicates the state of the muscle in the corresponding area of the body. It can indicate whether the person is overstressed or not.
Coldness and moisture in the foot	Fear and anxiety.
Strong odor in the feet	Digestive problems.
Skin peeling	An indication of the process of cleansing and renewal.

Foot Odor

Discussing foot odor is somewhat of a taboo in our society, but if our feet have a certain odor it can definitely be an indispensable clue about what system in our body is calling for attention. As a rule of thumb, there are five different odors connected with The Five Elements and five body systems.

Odor	Element	Systems
Rusty	Metal	Lungs and Large Intestine
Burnt	Fire	Heart, Blood and Small Intestine
Moldy	Water	Kidneys, Urinary Tract and Immune System
Sweet	Earth	Stomach, Spleen and Pancreas
Sour, Rotten	Wood	Fertility, Liver and Gall Bladder

Toe Positions

Forward Toes	A forward person. Optimism and vitality.
Retracted Toes	Closed, lack of expression, pessimism and defensiveness.
Toes with Gaps / Spacing Between	Needs freedom, independent, talented, sharing, can't keep a secret.
Tight Toes / No Gaps	Keeps secrets intimate, doesn't like exposure, open but not in talking about them.
Conjoined Toes	A link of two energetic centers: usually second and third toes, leadership and charisma.
Overly Relaxed Toes	Lack in resistance, traumatic event.

Raised Toes	Pride and condescendence in an energy center. Aloofness and disconnection.
Flexible / Bending Up	Flexible, energetic center with the ability to compromise.
Stiff Toes	Stubborn, holding on.
Twisted Toe and / or Twisted Toe Nail	A distorted energy center.
Toes That Overlap:	
When #1 overlaps #2	Too practical, values thinking over habits.
When #2 overlaps #1	Dominance, doing first and thinking later, values movement and habits over thinking.
When #2 overlaps #3	Repression of instincts in favor of practicality, anger and violence, values practicality over survival.
When #3 overlaps #2	Practical hypochondriac, anxiety, fanaticism and over practicality, survival and instincts over movement and habits.
When #3 overlaps #4	Instincts and survival over emotions, too courageous, emotional repression, emotional justification of fanaticism.
When #4 overlaps #3	Emotions over existentialism and instincts. Emotions suppress instincts, cowardice.
When #4 overlaps #5	Emotional center represses creativity and sexuality, creative art, repressive moods, mental or emotional conditions, stuck.
When #5 overlaps #4	Creativity and sexuality repress emotions.

Appendix VIII - Foods to Change to Balance Our pH

To Acidify the pH of Both the Urine and Saliva:	Corn Silk Tea, Watermelon Seed Tea, Yellow Dock, Apple Cider Vinegar, Ascorbic Acid, Cranberry Juice
To Alkalize the pH of Both the Urine and Saliva:	Chaparral, Lemon Juice and Water, Prune Juice, Apricots, Cauliflower, Corn
To Acidify Urine Only:	Arrowroot, Cornstarch, Popcorn, Walnuts, Corn Syrup, Cornbread
To Acidify Saliva Only:	Sauerkraut, Asparagus, Goat's Milk, Onion, Powder Potassium
To Alkalize Urine Only:	Black Cherry Juice, Apple Juice, Bananas, Acerola Powder, Ascorbate
To Alkalize Saliva Only:	Green Peas, Strawberry, Guava Juice, Complex F (Standard Process product)
To Acidify Urine / Alkalize Saliva	Red or Green Cabbage, Hominy, Whole Wheat Bread, Toasted Baked Beans, Cornmeal, Cottage Cheese
To Alkalize Urine / Acidify Saliva	Blue Cheese, Fresh Carrot Juice, Tomato Juice, Fresh Orange Juice

Appendix IX - Spinal Chart of the Foot

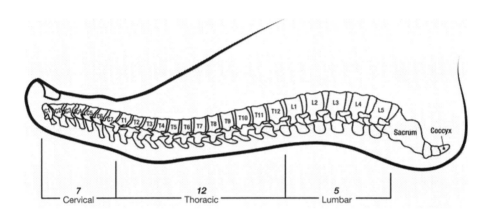

Appendix X – The Chakra Chart

#	Location	Characteristic	Color
7	Crown of Head	Totality of Being. Spiritual Perfection.	Violet
6	Forehead (3rd Eye)	Visualization. Psychic Sight.	Indigo
5	Throat	Communication. Creative Expression.	Blue
4	Heart	Universal Love. Compassion. Empathy.	Green
3	Solar Plexus	Creation of Self. Perception and Projection of Self. Conditional Love	Yellow
2	Sacral (Pubic)	Desire. Money. Sex. Creativity.	Orange
1	Base of Spine	Physical Vitality. Survival. Family.	Red

Appendix XI – Totem Animal Chart

Alligator	Integration. Represents a broad re-evaluation of a situation so that we can have a better understanding of what is happening now. Observe your healing process, life lessons and experiences so that you develop a more integrated sense of self.
Armadillo	Boundaries, Sensuality. Knowing where you end and others start. Helps to define and establish a healthy sense of boundaries in all interpersonal situations. With a healthy sense of boundaries our energy is not drained and we can enjoy a healthier sense of self.
Badger	Represents aggression and the courage to take action and seek new ways of expression. Connect us to the root of all things.
Bat	Death and Rebirth. Symbolizes the need to let go of parts of us that serve no more and embrace new aspects in our life.
Bear	Known for its period of hibernation, he represents introspection. Bear can help us with the ability to turn inward to access our strength and honor our nature cycles. He teaches us when it is time to act and when it is time to be still.
Beaver	Has an amazing ability to build and create. Beavers can help you solve problems by creating solid solutions. The ultimate Doer.
Black Panther	Carries the medicine that diffuses worry about the future. It makes us embrace the unknown and delve into it, knowing that in the stillness all mysteries will unfold.

Bobcat / Lynx	Represents secrets, the ability to unveil them and clairvoyance. Be receptive to messages and omens.
Buffalo / Bison	Brings abundance and healing. The buffalo is sacred to Native American people and no part of him wasted. He represents the power of manifestation through prayer. Be humble and ask for help. It always arrives.
Cougar	Symbol of power. Cougar teaches you to follow your heart and assume leadership for yourself. Cougar responds to any challenge with swiftness and without panic.
Coyote	Known as the trickster. He calls on us to look truthfully at ourselves and our behavior and actions, especially when sabotage is involved. Life unfolds better when we don't take ourselves too seriously.
Crow	Messenger, keeper of sacred law who sees with a unified eye (non-duality). Helps unite past, present and future into a new sense of self, purpose and mission. Helps us become impeccable and authentic.
Deer	Alertness, gentleness and a symbol of sensitivity and kindness. Helps accept others as they are and thus allow the change to happen through acceptance. Gentleness and compassion heal all wounds and the wounded through warmth and caring.
Dolphin	Messengers between water and sky. They are playful and intelligent. They bring the message of harmony and balance through conscious breathing. Dolphin connects us to the divine providence through rhythm and pattern.

Eagle	Symbol of freedom and perspective. As a representation of great spirit Eagle carries our prayers to the sky. He teaches us to give ourselves the permission to fly.
Elk	Teaches about stamina, the importance of pacing yourself enabling you to successfully complete your chosen task. Also, it may be time to seek the company of your own gender for w while for healing work.
Fox	Cunning and clever he moves with the utmost discretion. Fox teaches us to slow down and observe while being invisible through camouflage. He is the family unit protector.
Frog	Assists with the cleansing of our emotions. With the element of water frog shows us how to start afresh. It may be time to clean ourselves from any person. Place or event that serves no more our new sense of self.
Hawk	Symbol of observation and awareness. Be aware of messages from the Universe. Take a high stance to observe your life from a broader standpoint.
Horse	Represents strength and freedom. Horse teaches us how to use our power gracefully through sharing our gifts with others.
Humming bird	Joy, pure and simple. Joie de Vivre. The high frequency of Joy in all shapes and forms, including the highest aesthetics in art and music. Hummingbird calls us to drop our judgments and embrace Joy.
Mole	Explores below the surface by digging a little deeper therefore he helps us with our subconscious minds.

	Mole will help you explore the hidden parts of yourself.
Moose	Teaches us the sense of self esteem and to be proud of our accomplishments. Remind yourself of what you have achieved and what you like about yourself and others.
Opossum	Diversion. A symbol of the ability to get out of a tight corner using drama, imagination and strategy.
Otter	Master at enjoying life. Otter is playful and chatty. The otter reminds us that play is an important aspect to enjoying our lives fully. Allow life to unfold while embracing intuition and the feminine aspects of you.
Owl	Represents wisdom. Owl has amazing vision bringing the gift of insight. Owl medicine sees through others and allows for no deception or ulterior motives to reign. Pay attention for dreams and omens.
Rabbit	Symbol of fear. Watch what you fear as you may be inviting it. Rabbit help us reveal our hidden talents and fears. Get rid of all fears and doomsday projections. Be in the now!
Raccoon	Raccoon carries the medicine of helping the underdog. It represents sharing our energy and abundance with others.
Raven	Messenger from spirit world. He represents mystery and magic. With Raven the divine intervention is at full power!

Snake	A very powerful and rare medicine that symbolizes transmutation and the shedding of one's skin. Transmute a part of yourself that prevents you from being whole.
Spider	Shows us the interconnection of all life through the power of her web. Messenger of creativity and the ever expansive nature of life.
Squirrel	Prepared for anything that life may present. They are extremely adaptable and teach us to trust that with preparation our own life will be simple and safe.
Turkey	Give away. Represents renunciation of possessions for the greater good of others. Teaches non-attachment and the well being of others. Through Turkey's generous giving we can restore a sense of balance.
Turtle	A fine teacher of connection to earth and grounding. Its shell represents protection from negative interference from others – conscious and unconscious.
Whale	Record keepers of the ocean. They bring us the gift of telepathy and teach us the value of sound.
Wolf	Great teacher. He helps you find the answers within yourself. Associated with the moon, wolf will help you develop your intuition and develop a keen sense of self.

Appendix XII - Biorhythm Chart

Phenomena	Light & Darkness	Month	Seasons
Biorhythm Name	Day	Moon	Year
Duration	24 Hours	28-30 Days	365.25 Days
Resulting From	Earth's Rotation on Axis	Moon's Orbit Around Earth	Earth's Rotation Around Sun
How it Affects Biorhythms	Charges at Night	Affects High & Low Tide	Cycle of Life
Division	Dawn, Day and Night	New Moon Half Moon Full Moon No Moon	Spring – Bloom Summer – Ripening Fall – Leaves Falling Winter - Withdrawal

Appendix XIII - Examples of Mind / Body Connections

Body Part	Meaning
Blood / Circulation	How we circulate joy in our lives
Ears	Listening
Eyes	Vision
Face	What we show the world
Feet	Our understanding of reality
Hands	Doing / Satisfaction with what we do (work, etc.)
Heart	Center of harmony and happiness
Ileo-cecal Valve	Discerning between what does and doesn't serve us (what is nurturing versus what is toxic)
Kidneys	Fear, emotional processing and discerning
Knees	Ego, fear
Large Intestine	Release of Resentment and Forgiveness
Legs	Walking our Path
Small Intestine	Absorption of information on a subconscious level
Spine	Center of awareness
Spleen	Worry, obsessing and over contemplation
Stomach	Acceptance and absorption of information on the conscious level

Appendix XIV - The Seven Laws of Self Mastery

1. Fear-consciousness drains us. Replace fear with love. Do not fear pain. Our painful experiences are simply lessons in learning about love. To defy fear-consciousness cultivate courage. Do this by participating in bigger and more expansive endeavors than the limits of a survival-based life.
2. Un-judge yourself and others. The only way to induce change is by acceptance.
3. Un-accept codependence. Cultivate personal power by recognizing codependence in your relationships.
4. Nobody is perfect, accept imperfection and strive to do your best. Acceptance yields forgiveness.
5. Dissolve anger by forgiveness. Anger clogs the higher self and intuition.
6. The bigger the challenge, the more light and soul growth are hidden in it. All challenges are blessings in disguise.
7. Recognize that good and bad are limiting terms. Accept life as a sphere where everything exists on different degrees of the same goodness.

Appendix XV - 22 Spiritual Laws and Inspirations

1. Being thankful for an experience / challenge prevents the experience from controlling us emotionally.
2. Being thankful for an experience / challenge prevents the experience from forming a pattern in our life.
3. Being thankful for an experience / challenge allows for our higher self to comprehend and integrate the lesson inherent in it.
4. Family and friends often respond to us with conscious and unconscious prejudice because we may be unaware of our spiritual ties to them.
5. Once we become aware of the spiritual ties with people in our life, our souls are afforded more growth.
6. As our soul is afforded more growth from understanding the spiritual ties with people in our life, we can change the patterns that no longer serve us and attract new patterns based on Spirit and love.
7. Under stress we tend to imitate responses imprinted on us in childhood, primarily from before age 5.
8. Codependence hinders our growth. It prevents us from taking control of our life.
9. Guilt invites dependence. Guilt is giving away power and giving away control over our life.
10. The only way to give up control is to allow Spirit to intervene in our life by simply asking it to do so. Dependence will keep Spirit away.
11. Take full responsibility for your past actions, while acknowledging that you have the power within you to see your life as a Spiritual School. This will allow compassion for yourself and will free you from acting on guilt and repeating the patterns of the past.
12. Compassion is the highest attribute of mankind. We have a responsibility to nature: animals, plants, people, earth, and

water, to name some. Every time we act on compassion - a beam of light shines from us and to us.

13. Spirituality implies interconnectedness: Acknowledging our ties to each other in our mutual growth.
14. Interconnectedness: Whatever we do, think, say, believe and feel about others we do, think, say, believe and feel about ourselves.
15. The Universe loves simplicity. Love. Live. Laugh.
16. Thoughts create our life. Thoughts are not generated in our brain alone. We are simply an amplifier of thoughts that come from the Universe. Only the ego can create fear-based thoughts.
17. Embrace your life history as a soul choice. This takes you beyond good or bad, for the soul's modus operandi is Growth.
18. All our experiences are about growth, not blame. Embrace the life lessons inherent in your most trying experiences.
19. Soul growth hinders grief. Soul grief hinders growth. Grief connects to the lungs, the seat of the soul, and stifles them. The more we dwell on grief, the less growth we allow our soul.
20. Mentally, we can like or dislike someone. It is a fair choice. Spiritually, we can only love everyone for we are all interconnected.
21. The conscious mind dwells on emotions. Emotions can only be fear-based or love-based.
22. Similar attracts similar. Our future lays in our thoughts. Our thoughts yield our words. Our words create our life.

~Part IV: Glossary and Index~

Glossary and Index
Word Definitions and Page Notations

Abdominal Floor – 11, 29, 80
> The tissue that defines the bottom of the abdomen. Holistically, it is where unprocessed emotions accumulate to create an energetic blockage (Water-Earth boundary).

Acidic – 35, 36, 42, 43, 73
> A pH value fewer than 7.0. Acidity often equals toxicity. De-acidify = Detoxify. Acidity shows in blood, urine or saliva.

Adrenal Glands – 25, 41
> Endocrine glands above the kidneys that have anti-stress, anti-inflammatory and other functions. Holistically, the seat of Courage. Literally means, "Above kidneys." Courage (adrenals) is above Fear (kidneys). It takes courage to conquer fear.

AIDS – 49
> Acquired Immune Deficiency Syndrome, caused by the retrovirus HIV. Transmitted by exposure to contaminated body fluids such as blood and semen. An achronic viral auto-immune condition.

Alchemy – iv, 119
> The art of converting matter into other forms of matter.

Alexander the Great – iv
> A Macedonian ruler who conquered most of the known ancient world.

Alignment – iii, 15, 54, 64, 120, 177, 178
> The process of equalizing and harmonizing.

Alkaline – 35, 36, 42
>A pH value above 7.0. Alkalizing the body is synonymous with detoxification.

Allopathic – 52, 169
>Western pharmacological medicine.

Analogies – ii
>A result of processing similarities.

Arachnophobia – 69
>A strong fear of spiders.

Archetypes – 16, 80, 155
>Symbols often represented by universally understood models of a person, personality or behavior.

As Above, So Below - iv, 30, 56, 65, 71, 72, 75, 120, 219, 220
>A metaphysical principle that explains parallel realities.

Aspirations – 4, 36, 71, 209
>Deep hopes that line up with our spirit.

Astral – 115, 116, 118
>Of a dimension that is invisible. Sometimes referred to as spirit or aura

Astrology – 7, 20, 43, 120, 123, 128, 172
>The art of observing reality as aligned with the universe, namely through the planets.

Attachments – 4, 96, 163, 185, 213, 218
>Emotional leanings toward aspects of one's reality.

Autonomic – 41
Independent, e.g. autonomic nervous system.

Bach, Dr. Edward – 46, 123
An English homeopathic doctor that researched flowers as the soul of nature (Bach Flower Remedies).

Biorhythms – 126, 127, 239
A rhythmic biological cycle that affects one's function in various domains, such as mental, physical, and emotional activities which allows for balance through duality.

Body of pain – See Pain body

Camino, The – ii
A book by Shirley MacLaine. It describes her pilgrimage journey to Camino Santiago De Compostella, Spain.

Chakras – 56, 84, 99, 100, 118, 145, 152, 160, 178, 179, 210, 233
Energy centers in the body that correspond to organs, functions, frequencies and colors.. Chakra is a concept referring to wheel-like vortexes which according to traditional Indian medicine are believed to exist in the surface of the ethereal body.

Chlorinated – 35
The process of adding chlorine, usually refers to water.

Comfort Zone – noted frequently
A state in which we tend to stall and act within a non-challenging, limited sphere.

Common Denominator – 16, 63, 164
A value or trait that unifies a range of observations at the most basic level.

Compensatory Mechanism – 73
A process that entails making up for a lack or dysfunction.

Completion – 8, 74, 167, 221
Resolution of a challenge.

Conditional Love – 124, 209
A form of fear-based love in which love is offered only under certain conditions.

Consciousness – noted frequently
A state of mind that is rational and guides many of our daily decisions, where we receive input from the senses, analyze the facts and are strongly affected by the opinions of others.

Contemplate – 54
The act of taking a deeper look at things.

Contractive – 81, 97, 112, 125, 162, 190
A state that is lessening or shrinking in focus and awareness.

Crystals – 5
In reflexology, refers to crystalline accumulations in the feet that correspond to blockages in the mind/body system.

Deformity- 8, 28
A situation where a lack of formation or completion has occurred.

Density – noted frequently

The state of being subjected to gravity as well as not being able to see beyond one's subjective reality.

Detachment – 54

The act of severing attachments to people, places or things.

Deviations - 5

A state in which a detour from the norm has occurred.

Diabetes – Type I & Type II – 36, 226

Chronic condition of the body's failing to secret sufficient insulin. Holistically, insulin reflects our ability to circulate love and sweetness in our lives.

Diaphragm – 29, 42, 53, 200, 225

The tissue that separates the chest cavity from the abdominal cavity. The border between the Fire and Water element.

Dichotomy – 33, 68

The existence of dualities, often opposites.

Disassociating – 44, 95

The process of failing to remain present, often due to trauma.

Disconnect – 30, 37, 38, 44, 140

A severing of a link or a mismatching of a bond.

Dispositional - 30

Having to do with one's disposition, attitude or personality.

Doctrine of Signatures - 119
 A philosophy shared by herbalists which states that herbs that resemble various parts of the body can be used to treat ailments of that part of the body.

Dogma – 2, 141
 A set of rules that does not allow for flexibility and/or exceptions.

Dynamics – 25, 68, 97
 The mechanism within which things or people operate.

Edema – 48
 Retention of fluids in the body.

Ego – noted frequently
 The fear-based body.

Electromagnetic – 117
 An adjective that relates to the energetic charge of things.

Elements - noted frequently
 See Four and Five Elements.

Emotional Body – 21, 49, 64, 96, 135, 169
 The subjective part of the body that is tied to the ego and past life experiences.

Encompassing – 40, 50, 154, 192
 The process of embracing different aspects of a subject and/or reality.

Energy – noted frequently
Relates to the non-physical reality.

Energy Bank Account – 113
The "storage" of our experiences, thoughts and intentions.

Enlightenment – 6, 155, 182
The act of realizing one's purpose.

Epithalamus - 126
A segment of the middle brain whose functions of its components include the secretion of melatonin by the pineal gland (involved in circadian rhythms) and regulation of motor pathways and emotions.

Equilibrium – 17, 107
The ultimate balance on all levels – physiological, mental, emotional and spiritual.

Ethereal – 115, 116, 117, 118, 156
Relates to a non-physical dimension.

Etymology – 71
The source of a word.

Five Elements – 7, 8, 13, 220, 229
A model that explains reality and health as comprising of Metal, Fire, Water, Earth and Wood.

Flower Essences – 123
Energy-based medicine stemming from flowers.

Four Elements – 7, 8, 12, 13, 17, 28, 29, 199, 220, 222
A model that explains reality and health as comprising of Air, Fire, Water and Earth.

Frequency – noted frequently
A resonance that emanates from people, objects, planets, thoughts, animals, etc.

Freud, Sigmund – 16
A Psychologist who presented Psycho-Analysis.

Garden of Eden - 2
From the Bible's Book of Genesis as being the place where the first man, Adam, and his wife, Eve, lived after they were created by God.

Gout – 73
An acidic condition often found in the feet.

Heaven vs. Earth – 1
The dichotomy of "As Above, So Below."

Hemispheric – 18
Of the hemispheres, often relates to the two sides of the brain.

Higher Self – noted frequently
The Soul-based part of our consciousness. Often juxtaposed to the ego.

Holistic Medicine – ii
A form of medicine that attempts to relate to the patient in a more universal and interconnected manner.

Homeopathic - 46

A form of alternative medicine in which practitioners treat patients using highly diluted preparations that are believed to cause healthy people to exhibit symptoms that are similar to those exhibited by the patient.

Homeostasis – 36, 42

The process of the ongoing equalizing and harmonizing of the body functions.

Hypertension - 42

High blood pressure, possibly due to a faulty circulation of joy in the body system due to deep unresolved emotional problems.

Hypothalamus gland – 30

A master gland in the brain. Its most important function is to link the nervous system to the endocrine system.

Illusionary – 78, 138, 144, 161, 167, 188

The faulty identification of the ego with its self-induced perception of reality. This identification is a cause of suffering.

Immunity – 49, 50, 200, 223

The mechanism that allows for the body to identify and attack external invasion. Stress affects immunity.

Incarnation – 15, 116, 127, 200

The process of manifesting energy into matter.

Infinite – noted frequently

Of non-ending nature. The true source of love.

Infinity – 2, 139, 150, 156, 157, 158, 221
	The non-ending nature of things. Often relates to non-physical reality.

Integrated – iii, 6, 77, 234
	The process of blending together and harmonizing different aspects of our reality.

Intention – noted frequently
	An energetic driving force.

Interconnectedness – noted frequently
	The definition of holism. The one-ness of it all.

Intercostals – 42
	Between the ribs (muscles).

Intricacy - 74
	Complexity or having many aspects.

Isolation – 30, 37
	Separation of removing from other people or aspects.

Jacob's Ladder Dream – 16
	A dream in which Jacob saw a ladder going up to heaven.

Jing – 47, 72
	A portion of life force or essence believed to be the carrier of our heritage (similar to DNA). In Traditional Chinese Medicine we receive most of our Jing at birth and can continue to receive more through various methods including martial arts.

Joseph's Dream Interpretation - 16

In the Bible, Joseph was asked to interpret the Pharaoh of Egypt's dreams. Joseph said that the dreams foretell of 7 years of plenty followed by 7 years of famine and that Pharaoh should store food during the time of plenty for the time of famine.

Judeo-Christianity – 2

The continuum of Judaism and Christianity, as stemming from one source.

Jung, Carl – 16, 120

A psychologist who adopted a more universal approach to existence.

Kaballah – 56, 65

A philosophy that seeks to explain and connect humans to the forces behind creation.

Karma / Karmic – 64, 115, 118, 127, 128, 131

A term that relates to the set of lessons we chose to learn based on the notion that this life is a part of a soul continuum. We bring to each life a certain charge from other ones.

Kingdom of Heaven – 3

A term that related to a harmonious reality that exists on a higher realm.

Knowingness – 58, 141, 168

The notion that deep inside we carry the knowledge of almost all things that were and will be, and that we can tap into them.

Kirilian Photography – 117
A method of photography that attempts to expose energy fields.

Kirilian,Semyon – 117
The founder of Kirilian photography.

Lucid – 55, 109
A state of heightened awareness.

Light-consciousness - 96
Corresponds to Love Consciousness – choosing to come from love as opposed to fear.

Linearity - 2
A thought or action that lacks in multi-dimensionality. Not considering the interconnectedness that prevails in the Universe.

Lupus - 46
A systemic autoimmune disease that can affect any part of the body. In Lupus, the immune system attacks the body's cells and tissue, resulting in inflammation and tissue damage.

Malkhut - 56
Malkhut means Kingship and is one of the 10 sephiroth on the bottom of the Kabbalistic Tree of Life. It is associated with the realm of matter/earth/form and relates to the physical world, the world of forms. Divine energy comes down to Malkhut and our purpose as humans is to move that energy up the Tree of Life.

Manifest - noted frequently
To make evident to the senses, to materialize. Noted frequently.

Manipulation – 8, 11, 36, 55
The skillful use of the hands in various forms of bodywork.

Maslow, Abraham - 63
An American professor of psychology who created Maslow's hierarchy of needs. He stressed the importance of Self Realization and focusing on the positive qualities in people, as opposed to treating them as a "bag of symptoms."

Matter - noted frequently
A general term for the substance of which all physical objects consist. A common way of defining matter is as anything that has mass and occupies volume.

Melatonin - 126
A naturally occurring hormone , secreted by the pineal gland, which relates to our biological clock and regulates rhythms of several biological functions including sleep.

Metabolism - 73
Our bodies get the energy they need from food through metabolism, the chemical reactions in the body's cells that convert the fuel from food into the energy needed to do everything from moving to thinking to growing.

Metaphysical – iv, 2, 80, 106, 120, 138, 164, 192, 211, 220
This refers to anything immaterial, beyond the senses and not physical. More properly, "beyond" that which is physical.

Microcosm – iv, 53
A smaller system which is representative of a larger one.

Modus operandi – 21, 40, 50, 107, 162, 243

A person or thing's normal and habitual mode of operation.

Monitor – 2, 34, 138, 155, 161, 209, 210, 214, 216
The act of using one's senses for the purpose of maintaining and improving a situation.

Native American Shamanism – 83, 121
A system of beliefs and practices concerned with communication with the spirit world of nature.

Nervous system – 41, 49
A bodily system that coordinates the activities of muscles and organs from data received from the senses.

Numerology – 8, 21, 219
The study of the relationship between numbers and the character or action of physical objects and living things.

Old Testament - 2
The Jewish Bible and the first major part of the Christian Bible, covering events before the time of Christ. It is subdivided into the categories of law, history, poetry and prophecy.

Pancreas – 5, 65, 200, 229
A gland near the stomach which secretes a fluid which breaks down larger molecules into smaller pieces. The pancreas also produces the hormones insulin and glucagon which regulate blood sugar. These hormones are released into the cardiovascular system. Metaphysically connects to Self-Realization.

Pain body – Noted frequently
A memory we carry of our perceived experiences from this lifetime and other lifetimes. It often contains unresolved conflicts and ego-based perceptions. It is also referred to as body of pain.

Pan-human - 16
Representing all humans.

Paracelsus - 119
A Swiss Renaissance physician, botanist, alchemist, astrologer, and general occultist.

Paradigm – 44, 45, 96, 120, 140, 149, 164
The set of experiences, beliefs and values that affect the way an individual perceives reality and responds to that perception.

Parasympathetic Nervous System - 42
Part of the Autonomic Nervous System (ANS) which is responsible for the involuntary regulation of internal organs and glands. The parasympathetic system is responsible for post-stress function, stimulating "rest-and-digest" activities including sexual arousal, salivation, tears, urination, digestion and defecation.

Perception - noted frequently
The process of attaining awareness or understanding of the environment by organizing and interpreting sensory information.

Peripheral - 41
External; away from the center; as in the peripheral portion of the nervous system.

Permeate – 75, 90
To pass through or penetrate without causing rupture or

displacement.

Phenomena – 91, 93, 97, 99, 112, 119, 120, 167, 176, 239
An observable fact or occurrence often considered very unusual, curious, or astonishing by those who witness it.

Phosphate - 48
Any salt or ester of phosphoric acid.

Physiological – 30, 79, 88, 100
The science of the function of living systems. This includes how organisms, organ systems, organs, cells and biomolecules carry out the chemical or physical functions that exist in a living system.

pH Levels – 35, 48
In chemistry, pH is a measure of the acidity of an aqueous solution. Solutions with a pH less than 7 are said to be acidic and solutions with a pH greater than 7 are basic or alkaline.

Phoenix Rising Yoga - 36
Classical yoga and mind-body healing practice based on contemporary client-centered psychological theory.

Pineal Gland – 126, 127
Also called the "third eye" it is a small endocrine gland in the brain. It produces melatonin, a hormone that affects the modulation of wake/sleep patterns and seasonal functions.

Pituitary Gland - 30
An endocrine gland that is a protrusion off the bottom of the hypothalamus at the base of the brain. The pituitary gland secretes nine hormones that regulate a stable balance in our bodies.

Placebo - 46
A dummy medicine containing no active ingredient. Anything of no real benefit which nevertheless makes people feel better.

PNI (see Psycho-neuro-immunology)

Polarities - noted frequently
The separation, alignment or orientation of something into two opposed poles or either of the two extremes of such attributes.

Pragmatic - 17
Functional, practical, concerned with making decisions and actions that are useful in practice, not just theory.

Predisposition - 36
The state of being susceptible to a trait, disease or other health problem.

Pre-monitory – 16, 211
Anything that serves as a foretelling of upcoming events and challenges.

Primordial – 2, 11, 100, 156
The first, earliest or original characteristic of an organism.

Process (verb: to process) – noted frequently
A series of events that occur to produce a result, especially as contrasted to product.

Projection – 17, 49, 51, 79, 90, 154, 159, 186, 193, 233, 237
A belief or assumption that others have similar thoughts

and experiences as oneself.

Psyche – 11, 34, 49
The human soul, mind, or spirit as the central force in thought, emotion, and behavior of an individual.

Psycholinguistics - 64
The study of the comprehension and production of language in its spoken, written and signed forms.

Psycho-neuro-immunology (PNI) – 48, 49
The study of the interactions between behavioral, neural, endocrine and immune functions.

Psychotherapy - 64
The treatment of people diagnosed with mental and emotional disorders using dialogue and a variety of psychological techniques.

PTSD (Post-traumatic Stress Disorder) - 79
Any condition that develops following some very stressful situation or event; such as sleep disturbance, recurrent dreams, withdrawal or lack of concentration.

Realization – 158, 164
The act of realizing, figuring out or becoming aware.

Reciprocal - 35
A feeling or action that is mutually and uniformly felt or done by each party towards the other or others.

Reconcile - 2, 4, 18, 30, 53, 58, 168
To come to terms or agreement.

Reflex – 5, 25, 54, 173
    An involuntary and nearly instantaneous type of physical or energetic movement in response to a stimulus.

Reflexology – noted frequently
    A natural healing art based on the principle that there are reflexes in the feet (also hands and ears) which correspond to every part, gland and organ of the body. Through application of pressure on these reflexes, the feet being the primary area of application, reflexology relieves tension, improves circulation and helps promote the natural function of the related areas of the body. Holistically speaking, the feet represent our understanding of ourselves, others and life in general, therefore reflexology may improve this understanding, which is a major key for healing.

Religion – 3, 140
    A cultural system that establishes symbols that relate humanity to spirituality and values. Many religions have narratives, traditions and sacred histories that are intended to give meaning to life or to explain the origin of life or the universe through a particular morality, set of ethics or a preferred lifestyle.

Rescripting - 131
    Writing a new script or storyline for a past event or situation with the intention to dissipate their negative charge.

Resistance – noted frequently
    An oppositional motion or flow away from an influence, either positive or negative.

Resonance – 20, 50, 116, 160
    A process of matching energetic frequencies that have a positive effect.

Respiratory – 42, 47
The human respiratory system includes airways, lungs and the respiratory muscles. Oxygen and carbon dioxide are passively exchanged between the body's external environment and the blood.

Sabotage – 24, 77, 148, 235
A deliberate action aimed at weakening someone or something through subversion, obstruction, disruption or destruction.

Saboteur - 23
One who engages in sabotage.

Script Game – 128, 129
A method presented by the author in which one is guided to re-write and replace a painful past event with a more loving and thoughtful scenario about what could have possibly occurred.

Self-realization – v, 5, 37, 38, 64, 65, 91, 103, 158, 208
A spiritual awakening from an illusory self identity image (ego) to one's true, divine and perfect condition. In the physical body, the pancreas had a direct relation to self-realization as the organ that governs the marriage between Energy and Matter.

Sephirot / Sephirah - 56
The 10 attributes / emanations in Kabbalah through which the Creator reveals himself and continuously creates both the physical realm and the chain of higher metaphysical realms. They include: Wisdom, Understanding, Knowledge, Kindness, Severity, Beauty, Eternity, Glory, Foundation and Kingship.

Serotonin - 37
Biochemically derived from tryptophan, naturally occurring in milk, turkey and bananas. Serotonin is primarily found in the gastrointestinal (GI) tract, platelets and in the central nervous system of animals and humans. It is a contributor to feelings of well-being and is known as a "happiness hormone" despite not being an actual hormone.

Shekhinah - 65
In Kaballah, the dwelling or settling presence of God or divine presence anywhere, but especially in the Temple in Jerusalem. While one is in proximity to the Shekhinah, the connection to God is more readily perceivable.

Shirley MacLaine - ii
An American actress, dancer, activist and author, well-known for her beliefs in new age spirituality and reincarnation.

Smudge - 34
A bundle of dried herbs, most commonly white sage, usually bound with string and dried. Having a strong, pleasant aroma when burnt, it is used by native traditions in rites of initiation and purification.

Sodium - 48
An essential elemental most commonly known as table salt.

Soul-based – ii, 102, 116, 187
Originating in or from the soul or essence.

Source, The – 3, 63, 85, 97

The origin or beginning of life energy.

Speculating - 38
To theorize or take to be true, possibly without sufficient evidence.

Spirituality – 119, 140, 141, 243
An ultimate immaterial reality; an inner path enabling a person to discover the essence of their being; or the "deepest values and meanings by which people live."

Spiritualized – i, 85
Infused with spirituality.

Subconscious – noted frequently
The state of mind in which we are hardly aware. It is where our thoughts are unrestricted by logic; it is where we dream and where many memories live. It determines most of our thoughts and behavior. In the physical body connects to the abdomen.

Superconscious - 74
The state of mind where intuition and heightened mental clarity flows. It sees all things as part of a whole. It can readily draw solutions because it sees the problem and the solution as one, as though the solution was a natural outgrowth from the problem.

Sustenance - 12
The providing of support or nourishment.

Symbolism – ii, 16, 17, 24, 54, 119, 120, 179
The representation of a concept through symbols or the underlying meanings of objects or qualities.

Sympathetic – 41, 42

As in Sympathetic Nervous System, it mobilizes the body's resources under stress to induce the fight-or-flight response. It is also constantly active at a base level to maintain homeostasis.

Synchronicity – iv, 13, 58, 63, 80

The experience of two or more events that are apparently unrelated, and are observed to occur together in a meaningful manner.

Tabula Smaragdina / Emerald Tablet – iv, v

A valuable ancient text that contains the instructions for transmutations, both physical and spiritual.

TCM (see Traditional Chinese Medicine)

Thymus – 49, 50, 51

A lymph gland located behind the top of the breastbone. It is most active during puberty, plays an important role in the development of the immune system and produces lymphocytes.

Totem Animal - 120, 121, 122, 180, 234

Based on Native American spirituality, a totem animal guides us toward various characteristics expressed through the symbolism of each animal. Also called Medicine / Power Animal.

Traditional Chinese Medicine (TCM) – 7, 25, 47, 100, 201

The medical theory and practices of Chinese culture, especially herbal medicine, acupuncture and osteopathy, for preventing or treating illness and promoting health and well-being; abbreviated as TCM.

Transcendence – 84, 85
The state of being free from the constraints of the material world.

Transient - 96
Remaining only for a brief period of time, occasional, passing by or through.

Transformation – 21, 67, 129, 140
The process of changing greatly in appearance, nature, form or condition.

Transmuting / Transmutation – 80, 145, 238
To change, transform or convert from one form to another.

Unification – 2, 16, 84
Becoming one, the process of merging into one.

Universal Truths – v, 8, 64, 81, 96, 173
Widely held beliefs that transcend all philosophies, traditions, mythologies and religions.

Universe – noted frequently
The totality of everything that exists – one-version, all one.

Vertebrae – 36, 54, 223
Individual bones in the spinal column.

Viable - 129
The ability of anything to exist, survive or thrive.

World of Forms – 1, 29, 56, 83, 97, 116, 119
The physical essence of what we know as our world of substance. The World of Forms is bound by time and space.

Yoga / Yogi – 36, 45, 68, 146, 165
Yoga is a traditional physical, mental and spiritual discipline originating in ancient India. The goal is the attainment of a state of perfect spiritual insight and tranquility. A Yogi is a practitioner of Yoga.

Zodiac – 19
The universal cycle of 12 astrological signs / aspects that approximately correspond to the months of the year.

Made in the USA
Charleston, SC
11 August 2012